Contents

Figures

Introduction

Partnerships between
Marketing and
Futures Strategies

Future-Driven Library Marketing is about partnerships: the partnerships that can be forged between elements of marketing and appropriate futures strategies for libraries. The ideas presented cover new ground. While much has been written about marketing and planning as independent processes, both in general terms and also specifically directed to library management, the application of futures strategies to the marketing effort is an entirely new approach.

In a previous book, I proposed that the marketing and planning processes can be more effective if combined into a merged process.[1] I still believe that this is true, and the details are explained in chapter 1. In many ways, this merging creates a type of partnership between marketing and planning, resulting in an expanded marketing endeavor. However, the partnerships to be the primary focus of this book are those that link this expanded marketing process with selected futures strategies.

The concept of partnership is one of parity. Each partner brings a unique contribution to the relationship, and these contributions must appear to be in balance. In an effective arrangement, partnerships are enabling and have the following attributes:

provide for the division of responsibilities

increase the amount of energy and expertise available for problem solving and doing necessary work

create communication linkages to promote information exchange

stimulate an interactive environment in which the existence of the partnership is actually greater than the sum of its individual and independent parts

In other words, the goal of establishing a partnership is the improvement of an existing situation through shared resources. When library marketing is the object of discussion, then a betterment of the present process becomes the goal. The partnership presented in this book can be described as a simple equation:

$$F(m + p) = M$$

In this equation, F represents the potential assortment of futures strategies that can be appropriately applied to the marketing (m) and planning (p) merged processes that yield a more powerful marketing (M) result. Even the expanded marketing process can be improved; applying futures techniques can multiply the marketing impact.

Overview

As we examine future-driven library marketing, we need to begin with a discussion of marketing itself, within the structure of the merged marketing/planning approach. In chapter 1, marketing is presented as a management tool, with a detailed analysis of each element of the merged process. The following items are explained: the marketing audit, the library's mission, the library's products, goals and objectives, costing (price), distribution (place), action strategies, promotion, and evaluation.

Chapter 2 introduces the twin concepts of futuring and futurists. The definition of futuring centers on the identification of possible futures, with the intent of working toward the one that is preferred. Futurists are those individuals who care about the future and who develop strategies that help in identifying possible futures.

Libraries face a spectrum of potential futures, ranging from the bright prospect of becoming a major player in the information field to becoming less and less supported as a viable institution. For this reason, it is essential that librarians not only engage in efforts to market the library but also develop the perspective of futurists and work toward a desired future.

The next eight chapters illustrate partnerships between each marketing element and an appropriate futuring technique. Chapter 3 addresses the library's mission and relates it to the creation of a vision statement. The differences between these two documents are assessed and suggestions are given for coordinating the two statements. It is important that library staff create both statements, as the mission reflects the "now" and the vision statement speaks to what "will be."

Chapter 4 focuses on the marketing audit and explores using systems analysis to inform market research and the use of focus groups. This chapter takes a close look at market research and the various types of methods that can be helpful to library managers. Focus groups can be a particularly effective method of collecting data during a marketing audit, and the chapter details the advantages of using this approach.

The futures screen is the topic of chapter 5, and the importance of identifying and analyzing trends is explored. The strategy suggested for informing this process is the Delphi Method, a research technique first developed by the Rand Corporation. Relying on attributes of anonymity, iteration, and participant expertise, the Delphi Method can help to target what the future may have in store for libraries.

In chapter 6, the partnership lies between identifying potential library products and the futures strategy of scenario building. Scenario writing can become a fertile testing ground for visualizing library products in a realistic setting. Library planning teams develop scenarios in which each product is inserted and "tried out." Both positive and negative potential outcomes are suggested using the scenario technique.

Two futures strategies form the partnership with cost-benefit analysis in chapter 7. The "price" element of the marketing mix is defined as cost—the cost to produce each product. In this chapter, the costing exercise is observed via the prospect of demand. The lenses of trend extrapolation and cross-impact analysis are used to discover the relationship between cost and demand. By the conclusion of the chapter, the two lenses are combined into a unified approach.

Library products need to be connected to customers. This involves a variety of types of distribution ("place" in the marketing mix). In an electronic world, distribution channels are continually changing, and the decisions that need to be made regarding which channels should be used to reach which audiences are becoming more complex. Traditional distribution outlets are being changed by electronic access, and the important choices to be made can be informed by the use of decision trees—the future strategy partner highlighted in chapter 8.

Libraries are promoted via a wide variety of techniques, and the complete profile of promotional tools and technologies is changing rapidly. The Internet and the World Wide Web (plus technologies as yet unimagined) are having a profound effect on how promotion is accomplished. Technological forecasting and assessment frequently use a combination of futures strategies, many of which are introduced in chapters 3 through 8. In chapter 9, such forecasting and assessment methods provide insight into future possibilities and avenues of promotion. Science fiction is also considered as a useful (even practical) tool.

Chapter 10 focuses on evaluation of library services, beginning with a discussion of why evaluation is necessary and moving on to types of evaluation. The futures partner in this chapter is simulation gaming, suggested as a way to monitor progress throughout the marketing process. Evaluation asks these questions:

- Are we still on track?
- Why has this event been accomplished earlier (or later) than expected?
- If we were to begin again, what would we do differently?

Simulations can help library managers explore these questions.

The final chapter summarizes the thrust of this book in its title, "Learning to Live in the Twenty-First Century: The Future

Starts Now!" While I have attempted to introduce the reader to the benefits that can derive from linking futures techniques to the marketing process, the hoped-for outcome is a successful transition into the next millennium. It is but a short stroll to the next century, and the challenges facing libraries are unprecedented. With the rate of change increasing and new developments continually eclipsing older technologies, we live in a world in which libraries may—or may not—have a desirable future. By using strategies presented in these chapters, the library manager can assemble tools for dealing with these challenges and anticipating events while yet able to influence the future to the library's advantage.

Effective marketing is critical to a library's success. Future-driven marketing can make that success more possible. Ignoring the future can result only in a perilous tomorrow; working toward a preferred future is the key to making the library survive—and thrive—into the next century. It has been said that today is the future that we worried about yesterday. Combining marketing strategies and futures methods can make tomorrow that future that we planned for today.

THOUGHTS AND MUSINGS

What partnerships are present between my library and other agencies?

How effective are these partnerships?

How are responsibilities divided in our present partnerships? Is there parity?

What other partnerships might/could be forged?

What can I do personally to enhance our present partnerships? To seek out new partnerships?

Editor's note: Throughout this book, when a citation number appears at the end of an introduction to a list, the italicized items in the list are attributed to the cited source. Comments immediately following the italicized material are the author's interpretation or discussion of the material as it relates to the library field.

Note

1. Weingand, Darlene E., *Marketing/Planning Library and Information Services* (Littleton, Colo.: Libraries Unlimited, 1987).

1

"Marketing 101"

The Foundation of It All

In the library as everywhere else, marketing is a process of exchange: the exchange of elements of value between producer and consumer. In many ways, marketing can be regarded as a partnership that is established based upon this premise of mutual benefit. However, too often, marketing is defined in the literature in the language of promotion or of public relations. This is unfortunate because as important as the promotional function is to the marketing process, it is only one part of the total effort—one of the final parts. When a librarian's attention is limited to just this one portion of the entire marketing process, marketing is not truly taking place.

Philip Kotler, in his ground-breaking treatise on the marketing strategies so successful in the private sector translated into the nonprofit sector, created a model called the "4 *P*s."[1] These *P*s, as adapted and defined for the library profession, include:

> *Product*   those programs and services that the library provides to its customers

1

Price   what it costs to produce its product, plus any user fees that are assessed

Place   how products and customers (or patrons) are connected; distribution channels

Promotion   how the library communicates with its customers, relating details on how customer needs have been identified and what responses have been developed to meet those needs

A mnemonic device is created to help retain some concept in memory. Kotler's *P*s model is a useful tool when trying to remember the components of marketing. To this original model, I add two additional *P*s—*Prelude* and *Postlude*—to accommodate the marketing audit (Prelude) and evaluation (Postlude). These additions first appeared in a previous book, *Marketing/Planning Library and Information Services.*[2] Also presented in the work was the concept of combining the (now) 6 *P*s of marketing with traditional planning elements.

The Marketing and Planning Partnership

Planning is an essential addition to the overall marketing process—creating yet another partnership.

> There is an appropriateness about the convergence of the marketing and planning processes: either of these two processes, while having intrinsic value, is incomplete without the other in the sense that each amplifies the power of the other and provides a wholeness of purpose and application.[3]

However, there is an assumption that must be understood and accepted: that is, all decisions are written in sand and not in stone. This assumption of flexibility also undergirds the library's mission and role statements, and when the library's external and internal environments are analyzed, the data may suggest that a different mission and different roles may be appropriate.

The rationale for merging the planning and marketing processes is rooted in the need to make decisions within a logical, organized structure that has been developed with input from the community. Otherwise, librarians may find themselves in a cycle of reactive coping with existing and emerging crises. As the rate of change continues to accelerate, the insistent clamor of problems, demands, and urgent situations can become deafening, distracting librarians from any activity beyond the immediate. However, it is this very existence of persistent crises that presents a compelling argument for infusing managerial responsibility with the merged marketing/planning process. Moreover, this blending of marketing and planning with other managerial functions can be a strong deterrent to the emergence of a crisis. When advance thought and analysis are normal practices, problems are less likely to grow to crisis proportions.

The merged form of marketing and planning can be considered a framework. (See figure 1-1.) This schematic graphically shows how the marketing and planning systems fit together. To follow this diagram through, note that the processes move sometimes in a single direction and sometimes in several directions. The following sequence is illustrated:

1. An analysis of the library's *external environment* is conducted.

2. An assessment of the library's strengths and limitations *(internal environment)* is made.

3. The data from these two analyses become the *marketing audit*.

4. Following the marketing audit, the organizational *mission* is reconsidered.

5. Once the mission and appropriate roles are determined, the *goals* for the time period are established (one year for a short-range or operational plan and five years for a long-range plan).

6. An *analysis of trends* is made (environmental scanning).

7. *Measurable objectives* are developed that will move the library forward toward its goals.

8. *Products* (collection, services, and programs) are identified as the objectives are finalized.

9. An analysis of *price* (the cost to produce each product) determines product priorities.

10. *Action plans* that will accomplish each objective are designed.

Figure 1-1　The Merged Marketing/Planning Process

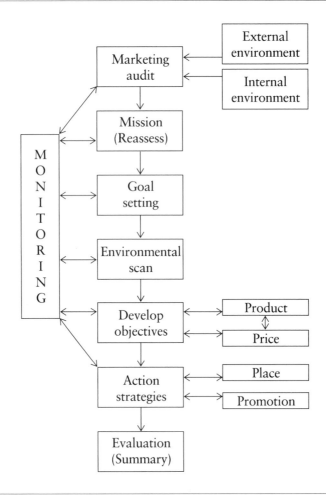

11. Distribution *(place)* decisions are made to effectively connect products with customers.

12. *Promotion/communication* channels are determined that will effectively reach the target audiences.

13. A final or *summary evaluation* and updating is made of all goals, objectives, and priorities. (Note: An ongoing evaluation monitors progress toward the goals throughout the process.)

It is important to emphasize once again that integration of the elements of the two processes, as illustrated in figure 1-1, provides a more reasonable and consistent approach to the marketing and planning efforts than either system employed independently. Planning sets the conceptual framework; marketing implements the planning directives and creates the desired environment.

The following discussion presents a brief overview of each element presented in figure 1-1. Fuller discussion of these concepts is presented in subsequent chapters.

The Planning Team

This marketing/planning structure should begin (although not depicted in the model) with the creation of a planning team, a working group composed of stakeholders (representatives of those customer groups who will be affected by the decisions to come). The team should consist of members from both the internal and external environments, so target markets must first be identified. The internal environment includes staff members from various levels, the policy board to which the library reports, and the library director. The external environment consists of customer groups that are served by the library, including funding sources and vendors. (See figure 1-2 for examples of categories of customers from which team members can be drawn.) The library director serves as ex officio resource to the team.

The final team roster may include quite a few names—frequently as many as nineteen or twenty. Therefore, to accomplish real work, the team needs to be subdivided into task forces. Each task force will focus on one aspect of the marketing/planning process. For example, one task force can develop or revise the mission statement; another can create a vision statement; yet a third can begin work on goals and objectives. Because of the volunteer nature of such team membership, it is important that one or more library staff members be assigned as staff to the team. This staff support might perform such activities as scheduling meetings, photocopying, taking minutes, and so forth.

A parallel group can also be created. Imagine an advisory group that includes the most influential and powerful people in

Figure 1-2 Possible Members of the Planning Team

Type of Library	Categories of Team Members	Whom Can I Identify?
Academic	Board of Regents Deans Faculty Students Academic staff Clerical staff Library staff	
Public	City/town/township/ county board Media Schools Small businesses Social service agencies Local organizations (for example, garden club) Service clubs (for example, Rotary) Clergy Library staff Students	
School	School board Administration Teachers Parents Students Clerical staff Custodial staff Library staff	
Special	Policy board Upper administration Department heads Employees Library staff	
Brokering service	Customers Competitors/partners Staff	

your community. Like the planning team, these people would also be drawn from a range of internal and external market groups. The key to involving such busy people is a simple one: *promise no meetings!* Instead, invite these prominent individuals to be part of an advisory committee to the library with the understanding that they can be contacted for advice, opinions, recommendations, and so forth.

Although community and staff input is frequently looked for in typical data gathering, it is less common for the planning group(s) to have such representation. Commitment and ownership can result from a process that ensures that those to be affected by decisions have been part of making those decisions. Planning groups that have a high degree of involvement not only contribute diverse perspectives but also endow the process with an atmosphere of cooperation and consensus-building.

Once the planning team (including the advisory committee) is formed, consider the planning cycle and its duration, or how often the process comes full circle and begins to repeat. Each year, as a new operational planning effort begins, review the long-range plan and revise it as necessary, forever extending five years into the future—a "rolling horizon" type of plan. However, if a major funding shift or significant community change occurs, the planning timetable may need to be revised as new environmental data are gathered.

Levels of Effort

The planning team must be realistically aware of the amount of resources (human, physical, and fiscal) that the library has available to devote to the marketing/planning process. Such an assessment examines the library's size, budget, and resources and determines the appropriate level of effort to be applied to each component of the process. Note that the proportion of resources does not need to be equally distributed across components. For example, in one year, the decision might be taken to focus resources on an in-depth marketing audit. This dose of realism can put the brakes on the temptation to do too much—and keep staff morale and enthusiasm high.

The following factors can be considered in determining an appropriate level of effort:[4]

> *Participants*   The more individuals and the more groups represented, the higher the library's level of effort for planning.

Resources   Higher levels of effort call for a greater commitment of the library staff's time and larger budget expenditures.

Library context   Libraries serving a community with rapid growth or change, a complex and diverse population, or shifting economic conditions or those libraries facing a major change in funding (positive or negative) may need to plan at a higher level of effort.

Planning purposes   What the library staff and community expect the planning process to accomplish may affect the level of effort chosen for some planning phases.

Planning structure   Libraries planning at a basic level of effort may approach many planning activities informally; however, as conditions become more complex, the planning structure will need to become more formal—increasing the level of effort.

Planning schedule   A less-complex planning cycle may be completed in a relatively short time; higher levels of effort may require more time to complete.

As introduced earlier, it is important to realize that the same level of effort does not have to be present in all phases of the planning process. If, as in the example given, a major marketing audit is done one year, another major effort may not need to be done for the next several years, and more resources can be directed to other planning phases.

The Marketing Audit

Both internal and external environments should be routinely examined. The internal environment includes the library's strengths, resources, and limitations; the external environment covers multiple levels but incorporates everything outside the library itself. (See figure 4-1 for examples of data elements in the internal and external environments.)

Kotler defines the marketing audit as a "comprehensive, systematic, independent, and periodic examination of the library's total environment, objectives, strategies, activities, and resources in order to determine problem areas and opportunities and to recommend a plan of action."[5] In other words, the marketing audit is a complex undertaking, yet one that is essential if library services are truly to respond to community needs.

A marketing audit covers both the assessment of customer needs and the attempt to understand community systems. Methods for identifying customer needs are discussed in detail in chapter 4. Such methods include surveys, interviews, and focus groups. Understanding community systems is perhaps less straightforward but of at least equal importance. Systems analysis is the futures lens through which the community is examined in the attempt to identify the flow of power, communication, and change.

In addition to this analysis of the external environment, the marketing audit analyzes the internal strengths and limitations of the library. Recognizing the relationships between what is presently provided and what is needed is essential to the improvement of library service. Learning what is needed—without determining the extent of the library's services and resources—is an incomplete exercise. By looking both outward and inward, the entire environment of the library is examined, with the intent of improving both library service and customer satisfaction.

The Library's Mission

Once environmental data are gathered through the marketing audit, the library's mission must be reexamined. Although every staff member holds a concept of what the library's mission should be, it is not uncommon for the new data to suggest that the mission and roles that are in place (even if only in people's minds) are not connected to community needs. This, of course, is one of the unstated side effects of seeking community input—the library must be prepared to respond to what is learned.

The mission is the library's statement of what it is about: what customers are to be served, what products are offered, what delivery systems are in place, and why the library is important to the community. It is brief, no more than a paragraph or two, and explains the library's philosophy of operation, stating what will and will not be done in the context of community needs and available resources. Figure 1-3 gives examples of library mission statements that can help to guide the planning process—and examples of statements that offer little guidance.

Figure 1-3 The Library's Mission: What Works and What Does Not

Mission Statements That Work

Mission Statements That Need Help

The Alpha Public Library serves the educational, informational, and recreational pursuits of the citizens of Brownville and its environs. The library offers materials in a wide variety of formats, presents programs on topics of local interest, and provides services designed to respond to community needs. In an increasingly changing world, the library seeks to position itself as the informational center of Brownville.

The Alpha Public Library provides materials, services, and programs to the citizens of Brownville. The library, as a part of local government, is accountable to the taxpayers of the community.

The mission of the Sinclair Corporate Library and Information Center is to serve as the informational center of the Sinclair Company. The library serves the professional and technical pursuits of the employees of the Sinclair Company. The library offers SDI (selective dissemination of information), individualized searches, and materials directed to the current and projected needs and interests of Sinclair employees.

The Sinclair Corporate Library serves the employees of the Sinclair Company and collects materials to meet their needs and interests.

The Greene Instructional Media Center serves the educational and informational needs of the students, faculty, and administration of the Greene Public School. The library's mission is to actively provide materials, services, and programs in support of the curriculum. To this end, continual interaction with school personnel and students is pursued.

The Greene Instructional Media Center supports the curriculum of Greene Public School and its faculty and students.

The XYZ State University Library supports the mission of the university and the needs of the students, faculty, and staff. In support of the curriculum, the library collects and delivers materials in a wide range of appropriate formats and operates as the information center of the campus. In cooperation with area libraries, it also addresses the intellectual needs of the surrounding community.

The XYZ State University Library provides materials and services in support of the curriculum of the university. It maintains a collection for the use of faculty and students.

Developing Goals, Objectives, and Action Strategies

Goals can be defined as statements of purpose or intent that are written in a general language. Goals, while flexible, are reasonably constant; at the same time, well-written goals frequently adapt well to changing situations. They may or may not be fully attainable. (For example, when would one fully achieve the goal "the library will provide effective information service"?) However, goals serve as a focus for continued planning.

Objectives are also statements of purpose or intent. However, they are written in language that makes them measurable and attainable, and they move the library toward stated goals. If "effective information service" is a goal, a related objective might be "To create a CD-ROM network by May 1999." Objectives are tools that demonstrate direction and respond to changing conditions.

The development of action strategies is the final step in this phase of the planning process. Each objective, in order to be accomplished, requires a series of completed actions. These actions are both concrete and detailed and are usually listed in sequential order. Like objectives, they are measurable; they contain a time line and denote who is responsible for their completion. In other words, action statements provide the working outline of specific tasks that must be executed before the objective is completed. Figure 1-4 gives examples of two sets of objectives and actions addressing the same goal—one set that is measurable and one that is not. It will be a very straightforward process to carry out and evaluate those objectives and actions that are measurable. However, the set that is not written in measurable terms will present a much more difficult prospect.

Environmental Scanning

The marketing audit can be viewed as a snapshot in time. It takes a picture of "what is" in terms of the library and its various environments. However, such a frozen profile is useful only to a point. It is also imperative that scanning of the environment—with special consideration of trends and subsequent alternative futures—is included in the planning process. It is not

Figure 1-4   Goal, Objective, and Action Strategies

Measurable	*Not Measurable*
Goal: To provide computer access in the library	*Goal:* To provide computer access in the library
Objective A: Have 3 computers available by October 1, 1999 (*Responsibility:* Reference Librarian)	*Objective A:* To buy computers for the library
Action 1: To investigate potential vendors and computer types by June 1, 1999	*Action 1:* Issue request for proposal
Action 2: Issue a request for proposal by June 15, 1999	*Action 2:* Make decision
Action 3: Make decision and issue purchase order by August 1, 1999	*Action 3:* Install computers
Action 4: Install new computers by September 15, 1999	
Action 5: Publicize and have open house by October 1, 1999	

unusual that, when an analysis of the community is done, the focus of interest is on the present, with little or no thought of what effect rapid change might bring. It is the responsibility of the planning team to gain information about trends and probabilities that may have an impact upon library operations. The process of environmental scanning seeks an outcome that has every probability of achieving the desired relationship of mutual benefit between the library and the community.

The Library's Products

Once the needs of the library's community have been identified through the marketing audit, the library's products can be determined. What are products? The concept of product has been transplanted from the for-profit sector and originally described those items that were developed by a commercial enterprise and then offered for sale. However, in the nonprofit library world, there are similarities that make the conversion reasonable:

In both sectors, there is intended interaction between producer and consumer.

The word *product* is derived from *producer,* and the library does produce a range of services.

The desired interaction is grounded in an exchange of commodities:

- In the profit sector, the exchange involves items or services that are offered for purchase.

- In the nonprofit sector, the exchange involves items or services that are supported by tax monies, contributions, or other support.[6]

A more-detailed discussion of the library's products can be found in chapter 6.

Price: The Costs for Each Product

Kotler's "Price" designation in marketing is often confused with charging a fee for service. However, while fees may be part of the picture for some product items, the primary definition of *Price* should be cost—the cost to produce each product item. There is no way to fully determine whether a product should be offered to the community without knowledge of the cost that is involved in producing and distributing that product. For example, for the product "interloan," a fee might be charged to help defray postage and handling costs; this amount is part of the price/cost profile for this product. However, there are also direct and indirect costs that need to be included, such as staff time, actual procurement costs, delivery, and so forth. Further discussion on library costing may be found in chapter 7.

Place: Distribution of the Library's Products

The next *P* to directly affect product decision making relates to how to connect each product with the target customers. Kotler refers to distribution as *Place*—a term that is relatively straightforward when the product is available at a single physical site.[7]

The concept of "Place" becomes more complex when there are several access points, such as those in a library setting, including both building(s) and other alternative delivery systems. Therefore, it is necessary to examine "Place" in the context of product distribution and connections between products and customers—with an emphasis on access. When access is held out as the operative goal, objectives and actions can be designed that will move the library toward providing distribution channels that meet customer needs in terms of time and point-of-use convenience. Obvious costs are connected to distribution and access, and specific judgments will need to be made as to which route(s) within a range of alternatives will be selected for each product. In chapter 8, distribution is again addressed, with special emphasis on electronic delivery.

Promotion: Communicating with Customers

Too often in the literature, marketing and promotion seem to carry the same meaning. However, it should now be clear that promotion is one of the final steps in the marketing/planning sequence and certainly does not drive the entire process. Rather, promotion is a collection of activities that communicate information back to the library's customers. At minimum, a variety of messages should be sent, including

- information about the library's mission, vision, goals, objectives, and so forth
- reporting of efforts to identify community needs and wants
- discussion of library products and how they relate to identified needs
- human interest stories about library staff and customers (with their permission, of course!)

In chapter 9, avenues of "spreading the word" are presented, with a focus on future-oriented technologies.

Evaluation: Two Approaches

Evaluation is an essential component of the marketing/planning process. Both monitoring and summary evaluation are required if marketing and planning are to be effective and meaningful management functions. The time spent at the front end of the process—assessing what information is actually needed for adequate evaluation to take place—saves frustration and wasted energy later in the process. Appropriate data collection should always be related to the desired outcome and must be linked directly to the question: "What do we need/want to know to make informed and intelligent decisions?"

Monitoring evaluation tracks the marketing/planning process through the one-year and five-year cycles, ensuring that the effort continues in the desired direction. It is somewhat like repeatedly checking a road map to be confident that one is still heading in the right direction. Normally, midcourse corrections are made, and each adjustment must be documented to make better estimates and decisions in the next round.

At the conclusion of the fiscal year, summary evaluation is done to address such questions as:

- Shall we repeat this project?
- What would/should we change?
- If we do something differently, what will it be?

Chapter 10 looks at the futures method of creating simulation games as a tool for evaluating library services.

Marketing/planning is, indeed, the foundation of it all. The partnerships between marketing/planning components and selected futures methodologies that are described in the following chapters are designed to heighten the effectiveness of each of these marketing elements. Preparing and implementing marketing strategies within the context of a futures orientation creates an overall partnership that is truly more than the sum of its parts.

THOUGHTS AND MUSINGS

What crises have occurred in my community in the past five years?

Were these crises viewed by library staff as problems or as opportunities? If viewed as problems, what opportunity factors can I identify?

In my community, who should or could I put on the library's marketing/planning team?

What level of effort is possible or reasonable for the library to expend in a marketing/planning process?

What portions of the marketing/planning process should receive the most effort? The least?

How could I help to increase the level of effort that the library can direct to the marketing/planning process?

Notes

1. Philip Kotler, *Marketing for Nonprofit Organizations*, 2d ed. (Englewood Cliffs, N.J.: Prentice-Hall, 1982).
2. Darlene E. Weingand, *Marketing/Planning Library and Information Services* (Littleton, Colo.: Libraries Unlimited, 1987).
3. Weingand, 16.
4. Charles R. McClure and others, *Planning and Role Setting for Public Libraries: A Manual of Options and Procedures* (Chicago: American Library Assoc., 1987), 4.
5. Kotler, 185.
6. Darlene E. Weingand, *Managing Today's Public Library: Blueprint for Change* (Englewood, Colo.: Libraries Unlimited, 1994), 132.
7. Kotler, 321.

2

Futuring and Futurists

*Working toward a
Preferred Future
for Libraries*

The future is an abstract concept through which human beings bring symbolic order to the present and meaning to past endeavors. Speculative pondering of what "might be" appears to be a key attribute of what it means to be human. Human coping strategies are often centered on the organization of present activities in the context of both past experiences and future goals. Yet, it is not until the last part of the twentieth century that research about the future in the academic sense has been formalized, moving this intense interest in the future beyond the role of the Delphic oracle or the religious prophet.

Today's speculations about the future have moved from the realm of fantasy or literary allusion into the pragmatic world of societal and institutional need to explore tomorrow to more fully understand the demands of today and the critical decisions that must be made. It is no longer enough to wonder what the future might bring; it is necessary to critically assess potential future scenarios and incorporate well-considered forecasts into today's planning.

The intent of this chapter is to examine the evolution of futures research, with special attention to its emergence as a serious research approach for use in the library. Specific methods are targeted that, while not an inclusive list of techniques, do represent a variety of approaches. It is important for library staff to become familiar with these methods that can help provide a clearer look into alternative futures. Finally, the chapter explores the benefits of incorporating futures research into library long-range planning, an additional managerial tool that will enable librarians to serve their communities more effectively.

Historical Development

The path between the past and the future has historically been perceived as a linear progression; in many cultures, the possibility of human intervention was not acknowledged, and the path was viewed as cyclical, recurrent, and predestined. For example, the Greek and Middle Eastern prophetic traditions set the stage for a vision of an unfolding future in which human actions became a significant factor in social improvement. Individual ethical responsibility displaced magic as dominant in the dynamic of change.[1]

Two key historical periods proved to be pivotal in the development of Western futures tradition: the Renaissance and the Reformation. The Renaissance produced the idea of scientific control over the environment through logic derived from observation and measurement of natural processes (for example, experimental evidence). In the Reformation, the idea of redemptive moral and social progress was organized in terms of materially evident grace and the deferment of more-immediate gratifications for long-term future gains. These shifts were most clearly observable during the Enlightenment when rational speculation about the future of the human condition became the prime vocation of the eighteenth-century philosophers. Utopian writers such as Mercier, Condorcet, Turgot, and others mark the beginning of "futures research."[2]

The growth of industrial society produced a new generation of "futures" prophets—such as Saint Simon, Fourier, Comte, and Marx—who commented on both social disruption and its potential for reordering society.³ However, although the nineteenth century can be described by a sense of material optimism regarding the future, it also became the beginning of a process of disenchantment—a perception that society might be approaching the boundaries of human capacity for change. The late nineteenth century and early twentieth century also heralded the emergence of the Utopian novel, notably in the work of Jules Verne and H. G. Wells.⁴

An example of large-scale direct linkage of futures thinking to long-range planning can be found in the Soviet five- and ten-year plans of the 1920s and 1930s. In addition, between the world wars, several new names (for example, Arthur C. Clarke and Buckminster Fuller) took center stage. Additional impetus occurred through social shocks such as those caused by the events at Auschwitz and Hiroshima. Concern with the future turned quickly into an attitude of social imperative. The launching of Sputnik in 1957 sent futures thinking beyond the scope of this planet, and a new reality was born.⁵

The roots of the modern "futures movement" can be traced to Europe in the 1950s where Bertrand de Jouvenel and Dennis Gabor emerged as early futurists. De Jouvenel was a well-known writer in the fields of economics and political science; his 1967 book *The Art of Conjecture* is regarded as a classic in the field.⁶ In the 1960s, de Jouvenel gathered together an informal group of scholars, known as "Futuribles," who met occasionally and published numerous articles on future political, social, and economic developments. Gabor received the Nobel prize for his invention of holography, and first examined the subject of the future in his 1963 book, *Inventing the Future*.⁷ Some of Gabor's early writings were intended as a warning of possible catastrophes that might occur unless there was timely intervention. In the early 1970s, the Club of Rome published *Limits to Growth*, which followed this line of reasoning.⁸

What Is Futures Research? Who Does It?

The simplistic answer to what is futures research might be: research done by futures researchers. But who are these people, and how does the library locate them? If the librarian is lucky, a staff member may have experience or interest in futures methodologies. A good first place to start is the World Future Society and its local chapters; membership in this organization is a clear indication of interest. However, such researchers do not fall into neat categories and, indeed, the question is further complicated by the following five statements:

1. There are no specific qualifications to be a futures researcher; a futurist is simply a person who either identifies himself or herself as a futurist or is so identified by others.
2. Futures research is not limited by the use of certain methods.
3. Although many people are concerned with, think about, or write about the future, only a portion of them call themselves futurists.
4. Futures research is generally not regarded as a field because its practitioners do not share a common academic background; indeed, it might be termed a "multifield."
5. Futures research is highly fragmented; it can, however, assist in dispersing intellectual fragmentation across other fields by focusing on broad, integrative work.[9]

Therefore, if futures research is difficult to label with a definition, perhaps a taxonomy of types of futurists can shed some light upon this complex question. Michael Marien, in an article in *Futures Research Quarterly,* divides futurists into two main categories: mainstream futurists and marginal futurists; a third category of non-futurist futurists encompasses pseudo-futurists and mythical futurists (confusing the public understanding of futures research).[10] Figure 2-1 provides a comparative view of this taxonomy, and the following paragraphs expand upon this figure. For the purposes of this chapter, only brief descriptions are reported.

The mainstream futurist typically tends to be a generalist and is identified as a futures researcher or professional futurist who attends futures conferences or contributes to futures journals. Six types can be listed; these are the

Synoptic generalist   an ideal classification, encompassing the ability to have a sense of the key elements of society,

Figure 2-1 Types of Futurists

Mainstream Futurists	*Marginal Futurists*	*Non-Futurists*
Synoptic generalist	Futurized specialist	Pseudo-futurist
General forecaster	Closet futurist	Straw-man futurist
Normative generalist	Future futurist	
Pop futurist	Forgotten futurist	
Multi-identity futurist		
Specialized futurist		

SOURCE: Michael Marien, "Toward a New Futures Research: Insights from Twelve Types of Futurists," *Futures Research Quarterly* 1, no. 1 (spring 1985): 13–14.

a grasp of trends and discontinuities, a willingness to forecast, a sense of plausible alternatives, comfort in dealing with complexity, a sense of values held by self and others, imagination, a theory of social change, direct or indirect optimism, and a sense of history

General forecaster   one who makes broad (in space) and long (in time) forecasts (not predictions) about changes in operating conditions

Normative generalist   one who makes no attempt to forecast the probable future but focuses on "alternative futures"

Pop futurist   the "popularizer" who writes for a broad audience, introduces people to futures thinking, and attracts people to using futures research or becoming futures researchers

Multi-identity futurist   similar to the pop futurist; one who is well-known and influential but is also known by other labels and with whom the futurist role may be secondary

Specialized futurist   a specialist in a single problem area, perhaps borrowing a few general forecasting ideas

The marginal futurist group has four subsets:

Futurized specialist   one who is only secondarily a futurist; someone who is interested in futures-relevant questions,

attends futures conferences, and contributes to the literature but who identifies primarily with another field such
as medicine, law, physics, etc.

Closet futurist   one who seriously thinks and writes about
the future but is in no way associated with futures research or the "futures movement"

Future futurist   one who will become a futurist at a later
time; possibly a student

Forgotten futurist   a writer or thinker from the past who
dealt with futures themes but was not regarded as a futurist

Two categories of non-futurist futurists can be listed:

Pseudo-futurist   one who employs the language of the future but offers no useful insight as to what might happen
or what desirable futures to pursue

Straw-man futurist   a nonentity that is never defined; a
conceptual and rhetorical target

It is easy to appreciate the confusion that surrounds futures
research and researchers. Yet, in a world—and a library—trying
to maintain balance in a time of out-of-control change, the importance of creating order in the midst of definitional chaos is
critical. Through sifting and winnowing, much of the chaff can
be eliminated. What remains is the core kernel of need—and a
mandate to develop useful strategies that will inform today's decision making. Certainly, the future will happen anyway; the
question is whether it is the future that the library prefers.

Futures Research as a Strategy
for Understanding Change

On a global scale, there appears to be a shared agreement that
society is experiencing a period of unprecedented change. Both
the substance and pace of change are fundamentally different
from what has occurred in past decades and centuries. No
longer are sequences of events occurring in relative isolation
over longer spans of time. As futurist John McHale proposes,

no longer are discrete groups of people affected by each change; rather, there is greater simultaneity of occurrence, swifter inter-penetration, and increased feedback of one set of changes upon another. Although the origins of many changes have roots in the past, McHale states that there are two critical aspects that have become dramatically visible within this century.

> One is the explosive growth in actual and potential capac-ities to intervene in the larger processes that govern col-lective survival. Global in scale, capable of affecting the physical balance of planetary life and reaching into indi-vidual human lives and societal institutions, today's change patterns now constitute a social and ecological transformation of unprecedented magnitude.

> The second is the severe lag in the conceptual grasp of this transformation and in the cognitive and affective under-standing of the processes through which change may be managed more humanely and effectively.[11]

What are some characteristics of change? Earl Joseph, noted fu-turist, argues that change

- alters something over time
- has a direction, rate of alteration, and curvilinear trajectory
- is caused by something
- can cause displacements
- can result in developing something new
- can have short-term positive or negative impacts
- has forecastable aspects of rate, magnitude, direction, and timing
- can have long-term consequences
- often is irreversible
- poses problems, threats, or opportunities
- is usually progressive
- accelerates in amount as society's knowledge base advances

- has a trend path precursor and a path into a future
- can be identified, researched, and forecasted[12]

The conceptual scope of change is difficult to grasp. While these characteristics seem to define what change is and what it can affect, the reality is that the change facing society today is beyond the set of skills most people have learned to use. The rate of change, formerly slow and sporadic, has never been so constant and overwhelming. However, reactive coping can no longer suffice; anticipating change has become critical to human survival. This is true not only for individuals but also for institutions. Traditions, standard operating procedures, and goals and objectives of every institution have been subjected to great stress as the result of accelerated and uncertain change. Modern managers must prepare their organizations for the trauma of unprecedented change; libraries are no exception. To effectively anticipate what is to come, we need to develop knowledge of futures research. Frederick Brodzinski states that by adopting a futurist perspective, library managers can be prepared for a variety of alternative futures and be better able to adapt to rapid and unpredictable changes in their environments, markets, and constituencies.[13]

What is a futurist perspective? Brodzinski identifies five principles, within the caveats that futures research techniques are no better than the data they use and that the futurist perspective must not be constrained by institutional traditions, values, and taboos.[14]

1. *The future is determined by a combination of factors, not the least of which is human choice. What we decide today will have a significant effect tomorrow.*

   The library that focuses energies and resources only on the present, without identifying and working toward a preferred future, is mortgaging that future.

2. *There are alternative futures. There is always a range of decision and planning choices. We must seek out and determine these choices and select the best possible alternative.*

   Many roads can be taken; a proverb states that "if you don't know where you are going, any road will take you there." It is critical that all choices are identified and that conscious, well-thought-through decisions are made.

3. *We operate within an interdependent, interrelated system. Any major decision, development, or force that affects any part of the system is likely to affect the entire system. We must be aware of changes not only in our own areas but in other areas within the system.*

   The library's system includes its parent institution, its customers, its internal strengths and limitations, and environmental forces. Decisions that are taken have ramifications both inside the library and beyond it. Therefore, it is urgent that outcomes and consequences for each decision be part of the decision-making process.

4. *Tomorrow's problems are developing today. Minor problems ignored today may have catastrophic consequences five years from now. Gradual changes or distinct trends and developments cannot be ignored. We cannot allow ourselves to become preoccupied with immediate concerns. The near future must be an integral part of current decision making.*

   This is another way of saying that we must look to the forest and not just the trees. If the library staff become so focused on immediate tasks and crises that they forget to plan, then the problems of tomorrow will develop unaddressed. In a time when change was gradual and slower paced, this was a lesser concern; today, it is a recipe for disaster.

5. *We should regularly develop possible responses to potential changes. We should monitor trends and developments and not hesitate to use the collective creativity and judgment of our staffs to develop forecasts, projections, and predictions.*

   Perhaps the Roman god Janus would be a good symbol for every library staff meeting: one face looking backward to appreciate and learn from the past, and one face looking forward in anticipation of what is to come. Even with all the futures research methods, there is no way to be certain of what the future holds. The challenge here is to use collective wisdom, in the light of identified possibilities, to move confidently into unexplored days, weeks, months, and years.

Once a futurist perspective, or mindset, is adopted, then futures research can be employed to gather necessary data.

The Case for Using Futures Methodologies in the Library

The way people think about the future has changed dramatically in recent years. A new attitude has emerged in public and private planning agencies as well as in the research community. The effect has been to extend former planning horizons into a more-distant future and to replace haphazard intuitive gambles, as a basis for planning, by systematic analysis of the opportunities the future has to offer. Societies and journals that focus on the future as well as conferences that are attended by thousands of people have emerged worldwide.

This change in attitude toward the future is becoming evident in the following three areas:[15]

> *Philosophically*   There is a new understanding of what it means to talk about the future. There is a growing awareness that much can be said about future trends in terms of probability, and through proper planning, considerable influence can be exerted over these probabilities. Moreover, it is recognized that there are many possible futures, with associated probabilities that can be estimated and manipulated. If the library's future is to be one that is both positive and proactive, it is essential to envision those futures that are desirable.

> *Pragmatically*   There is a growing recognition that it is important to do something about the future. This new attitude derives from the perception that not only are technology, society, and the environment undergoing change but that the rate of change is accelerating. Therefore, it has become necessary to strive to anticipate change proactively—rather than belatedly reacting to change that is already occurring. Library staff must not only visualize how the future can and should look but must also strive to make such a future a reality.

Methodologically There are new and more effective ways to do something about the future. Futures research—which seeks to explore the potentialities of interactive intervention in future developments—is emerging as a highly multidisciplinary branch of operations research. It is important that librarians add a variety of futures methods to their complement of management tools.

After becoming aware of what futuring is all about, of what futurists actually think and do, and of the importance of being proactive in working toward a preferred future, the next step is to consider some of the many methods that have been developed to connect with the future in tandem with the elements of the marketing mix.

THOUGHTS AND MUSINGS

What are some alternative futures for my library?

Which of these futures do I prefer?

In practical terms, how do I see my library's future . . . and my place in it?

Would/could I consider myself a futurist?

If yes, what kind am I? If no, how could I become more futures-oriented?

What changes have occurred in my community in the past five years? How has my library responded to these changes?

Notes

1. Jib Fowles, ed., *Handbook of Futures Research* (Westport, Conn.: Greenwood, 1978), 6.

2. Fowles, 6.

3. Charles Fourier, from France, was a founder of a utopian colony in the New World.

4. Fowles, 7.

5. Fowles, 8.

6. Bertrand de Jouvenel, *The Art of Conjecture* (New York: Basic Books, 1967).

7. Dennis Gabor, *Inventing the Future* (New York: Knopf, 1964).

8. D. Meadows and others, *The Limits to Growth* (New York: New American Library, 1972); Olaf Helmer, *Looking Forward: A Guide to Futures Research* (London: Sage Publications, 1983), 19.

9. Michael Marien, "Toward a New Futures Research: Insights from Twelve Types of Futurists," *Futures Research Quarterly* 1, no. 1 (spring 1985): 13–14.

10. Marien, 15–29.

11. John McHale, "Futures Critical: A Review," in Special World Conference on Futures Research, *Human Futures: Needs, Societies, Technologies* (Guildford, Surrey, U.K.: IPC Business Press, 1974), 13.

12. Earl C. Joseph, "Some Thoughts on Change," *Future Trends* 25, no. 3 (May–June 1994): 1.

13. Frederick R. Brodzinski, "The Futurist Perspective and the Managerial Process," *Utilizing Futures Research* (New Directions for Student Services, No. 6, 1979), 18–19.

14. Brodzinski, 20–1.

15. Helmer, 18–19.

3

*

Visioning

Creating Tomorrow's Mission

As individuals growing up, we must think deeply about who we are, what we want out of life, and where we fit in the grand scheme of things. Organizations are no different. The library's relationship to its community depends upon the philosophy of service that is developed over time with attention to these questions:

What does the library mean to the staff and to its customers?

What do the library staff members and the library's customers expect from the library?

Where does the library "fit" in the overall community environment? Where does the staff want it to fit? Does the community share this view?

These are serious questions, and they form the foundation for the philosophy of service that undergirds the library's operations and translates into the library's mission. Figure 3-1 presents scenarios in which these questions are answered for two very different libraries.

Figure 3-1   Two Scenarios about Service Philosophy

Questions	Scenario One	Scenario Two
What does the library mean to the staff?	A place for users to check out books	A window to the world of information
What does the library mean to its customers?	A place where materials can be checked out	The first place to check for information
What does the library staff want for the library?	Good funding and support	To serve community needs
What do the library's customers expect from the library?	Convenient hours	24-hour access
Where does the library "fit" in the overall community environment?	A "nice" place to visit but not an essential element of the community	An essential information resource
Where does the staff want it to fit?	Important to users and worthy of adequate support	Central to customer information seeking
Does the community share this view?	No	Yes

This chapter explores aspects of the library's mission and its vision statement. The differences between the mission and vision are also clarified.

A Definition of Mission

Reduced to its essence, the mission statement addresses the following components:

- *Why* is the library in existence?
- *Who* does the library serve?
- *What* products does the library offer?
- *When* can the library be used—and *how* (points of access)?
- *Where* is the library going (marketing/planning process)?

For anyone who has studied newswriting or journalism, these italicized words will seem very familiar; the same words are answered in the lead paragraph of most news stories. The mission statement also addresses these questions in a sequence of sentences or short paragraphs that attempt to explain the library's *raison d'être*—and more. Figure 3-2 presents scenarios for two different libraries that view the answers to these questions quite differently.

Often underrated as a component of the marketing/planning process, the mission statement is more than just a simple declaration of scope, audience, and intent; the mission must also incorporate a statement of service philosophy that can evolve naturally into library practice. In many ways, developing a meaningful mission statement may take more time and involve more discussion than any of the more pragmatic steps that follow. The importance of the library's mission should be highlighted, and sufficient time must be allocated to its shared development among all members of staff.

Figure 3-2　Two Scenarios about Elements of the Mission Statement

Questions	*Scenario One*	*Scenario Two*
Why is the library in existence?	To serve customer needs	As a community resource
Whom does the library serve?	The community, and especially target markets	Users
What products does the library offer?	Information and materials in a range of formats, services, and programs	Mostly books, some AV
When and how can the library be used?	24 hours a day electronically; during posted hours that reflect customer convenience	During posted hours at the physical site
Where is the library going?	It will become central to community information needs	It will publicize library materials and activities to the community

However, too many mission statements are primarily internally focused on staff goals and products: what the library will and will not do and what it will and will not provide. The mission statement that will move a library vigorously and successfully into the next century will shift that focus from internal operations to an *external* service strategy—with customer interests and preferences as the driving forces.[1] This is a matter of both philosophy and paradigms. (The connection with paradigms will be discussed later in this chapter.)

Mission and
the Philosophical Continuum

A philosophical continuum exists that ranges from the conservative position of the library as building/warehouse of materials to the proactive position of library as the sum of its services in an advocacy mode. The approach to customer service offered runs parallel to this continuum, extending from a bare minimum to the approximation of excellence. The following sequence illustrates the effect of philosophy on service rendered and is summarized in figure 3-3:

> *Most conservative*   The library is a physical location (building or room) to which customers come for materials and information. There are specific hours of operation. Materials tend to be in traditional formats. Staff operates within the physical site.

> *Mid-range*   The library is a physical location but also may be reached through alternative means (telephone, computer access, and delivery). Hours of operation are tailored as much as possible to customer convenience. Materials are available in multiple formats. Staff operates at the physical site but also has some involvement with the community served.

> *Most proactive*   The library can be accessed through an increasing number of points of access (physical, electronic, etc.). Customer convenience is foremost in deter-

Figure 3-3   Continuum of Library Philosophies

Most Conservative	*Mid-Range*	*Most Proactive*
Physical location	Physical location	Multiple points of access
Customers come	Alternative access	
Specific hours	Hours reflect customer convenience	Customer convenience foremost
Traditional formats	Multiple formats	Expanding range of formats
On-site staff	Staff on-site	Staff actively involved in community
	Some staff involvement in community	Referral to other agencies
		Advocacy

mining how, when, and where customers interact with library services. Materials are available in an expanding range of formats. Staff is actively involved in the community with responsibilities both inside and outside the library facility. Advocacy is a normal part of service, with the library staff regularly referring customers to appropriate agencies and checking on whether the need has been satisfied.

This spread—from a physical site to which customers come to that of the library as vigorous advocate for customer needs—constitutes a continuum with many points of intersection. The decisions that are made, even subconsciously, to place the library somewhere on that continuum have inevitable consequences that are reflected in how library operations are managed. During the marketing/planning process, one of the more challenging tasks is the development of a mission statement that puts into words where the library falls along the continuum. As stated previously, this phase of the process frequently takes up the greatest amount of staff time. Any young person knows that figuring out one's identity, goals, and role in life takes time, but the results are worth it!

The Connection to Paradigms

Another very important aspect to understanding mission development is the recognition of how one's philosophy is closely tied to the concept of paradigms. A paradigm can be defined as "a pattern or model that elicits behavior, together with the rules and regulations that we use to construct those patterns." Joel A. Barker, a noted futurist, notes that we use these patterns to establish boundaries and, ultimately, to direct us on how to solve problems that lie within those boundaries.[2]

Paradigms, therefore, influence perceptions, and the philosophy that emerges falls within the boundaries of the perceived paradigm. Barker has identified the following six important points, each of which is followed by further comment specifically connecting the point to the library situation.[3]

1. *Paradigms are common in all aspects of life.*

   The library is also governed by a paradigm. The notion of a hushed space, filled with books and staffed by (predominantly) women who wear their hair in buns, wear glasses, and say "Shh," is a paradigm that has been part of the popular mind for decades.

2. *Paradigms are useful; they show us what's important and what's not. They help us find important problems and go on to give us rules to help us solve the problems; they focus our attention.*

   This paradigm helped to define the library as a quiet space, useful for personal study and full of the knowledge of centuries.

3. *Sometimes a paradigm can become* the *paradigm: the only way one can do something. When confronted with an alternative idea, we reject it out of hand.*

   The question that must be asked is whether this paradigm is blinding many of us to alternative paradigms that are emerging and that may be more appropriately in tune with a changing environment.

4. *The people who create new paradigms are usually outsiders; they are not part of the established paradigm community and are not invested in the old paradigm.*

As our world becomes more global, linked with sophisticated communications technologies, many "outsiders" are becoming part of the information industry. Private vendors representing communications and computing are eagerly seeking a market share in what is regarded as an expanding and lucrative market. They have no vested interest in supporting or maintaining libraries as they perceive them (the old/present paradigm).

5. *Those practitioners of the old paradigm who choose to change to the new paradigm early in its development are paradigm pioneers. They have to be very courageous; the evidence provided by the new paradigm does not prove that they should be changing.*

The library profession has its share of paradigm pioneers. These library staff members envision the library as a key component in the new information society and seek to establish partnerships with other information providers. They work hard toward reframing the library's mission and operations to successfully make the transition to the new paradigm in which librarians serve as information mediators and electronic library access is the norm.

6. *You can choose to change the rules and regulations—shrug off one paradigm and adopt a new one.*

If a library is to be governed by the boundaries of the new paradigm, central to the community that it serves, the staff must consciously make those choices that will move the library from one paradigm to the other. This is not a simple case of decision making; rather, it involves reexamining every facet of library operations, from the mission statement itself to policies and procedures. Paradigms are powerful boundaries, and it takes a concerted effort to negotiate the transition.

Barker believes that changing a paradigm means fundamentally changing the way we do business plus learning new ways to solve problems. Further, he claims that paradigms act as filters that "screen" data coming into the mind, with the result that only data agreeing with the present paradigm are allowed to enter.[4] For example, data collected in a community survey may strongly indicate that customers prefer longer hours, weekend hours, and so forth. A staff member operating within the boundaries of the old paradigm may not "see" the data or, with his or her filter in place, may dismiss the finding as not relevant or possible in present economic circumstances. This is the "paradigm effect" in action, where the incoming data are screened, and present expectations dominated by the old paradigm keep the staff from anticipating and preparing for the future. The result is "paradigm paralysis" and the status quo.[5]

To move beyond the "paradigm effect" and "paradigm paralysis," Barker poses a question and recommends referring to it often: "What today is impossible to do in your business, but if it could be done, would fundamentally change what you do?"[6] This is a question that is central to developing not only a mission statement that incorporates enough latitude to move the library into a new paradigm but also serves as a springboard toward the creation of a dynamic vision statement.

Futures Strategy: The Library's Vision

If the library's mission can be viewed as a philosophical statement of what the library is all about—today—then the vision statement goes beyond today and focuses on tomorrow—what the library will be in the future. Too often confused, the mission and vision statements have very different purposes. While many libraries have developed some variation of a mission statement, locating statements of vision is a more difficult task. It is too easy for library staff to remain rooted in present crises and problems to be solved; it takes a concerted effort to rise above present issues to create a profile of tomorrow's library.

The literature is rich with examples of how vision is central to the welfare of individuals, groups, organizations, and civilizations. Viktor Frankl, an Austrian psychologist who survived the death camps of Nazi Germany, observed others who shared the ordeal and concluded that the most significant factor responsible for survival was the conviction that there was a mission to perform, some important work left to do—a personal sense of vision.[7] Others have noted similar positive outcomes. Children with "future-focused role images" perform far better scholastically.[8] Teams and organizations with a strong sense of mission outperform those without the strength of vision.[9] Even the success of civilizations is influenced by the "collective vision" people have of their future.[10] Therefore, it seems reasonable to propose that long-term success is dependent to a great extent on the shared vision that exists—or can be developed—in the minds of the library's stakeholders.

In their best seller, *First Things First: To Live, To Love, To Learn, To Leave a Legacy,* Stephen Covey, A. Roger Merrill, and Rebecca R. Merrill state that

> Vision is the best manifestation of creative imagination and the primary motivation of human action. It's the ability to see beyond our present reality, to create, to invent what does not yet exist, to become what we not yet are. It gives us capacity to live out of our imagination instead of our memory.[11]

However, one must know the parameters of present reality to move beyond it. This is where mission and vision intersect and interact. The vision statement should not be completely unrelated to the mission, but it should demonstrate how it builds upon the mission as scenarios are built for the future. Figure 3-4 illustrates the relationship between mission and vision.

Yet, vision is more than an extension of mission. *First Things First* discusses the "passion of vision," a sustained energy that clarifies purpose, gives direction, and empowers us to perform beyond our resources. In addition, the passion of shared vision empowers people to transcend petty, negative interactions—with a transforming, transcending impact.[12] While the book focuses on the individual, such ideas can be reframed in terms of organizations in general and the library specifically. The book gives eight characteristics of an empowering statement, which are restated here in a library organization context.[13] The vision statement

Figure 3-4   Comparison between Mission and Vision

	Mission	*Vision*
WHO	Serve the community	Serve the customer above all else
WHAT	Provide materials and services	Serve as the community's window to the world of information
WHEN	During posted business hours	Focus on customer convenience
WHERE	In library building and via telephone	Eliminate distance between products and customers
HOW	Provide materials, meeting space, study space, etc.	Take advantage of technologies as they develop
WHY	To serve the educational, informational, and recreational needs of the community	To serve as the information center of the community

1. represents the deepest and best within the library and the staff, coming out of a solid connection with the library's mission

2. is the fulfillment of the library's strengths and the expression of the library's unique capacity to contribute to its community

3. is transcendent and based on principles of contribution and higher purpose

4. addresses and integrates all four fundamental human needs and capacities: physical, social, mental, and spiritual dimensions

5. is based on principles that produce quality-of-life results

6. deals with both vision and principle-based values, what the library wants to be and wants to do

7. deals with all the significant roles that are appropriate vis-à-vis the library's community

8. is written to inspire the library's stakeholders, both internal and external

Creating and living such a statement has a significant impact on time management, focusing on years rather than minutes. It provides a sense of the library's unique capacity to contribute and prompts us to use compasses instead of clocks.[14]

Creating a Vision Statement

One of the ways to create a vision statement that will have real impact is through collaboration. Pennsylvania State University professor Barbara Gray sees collaboration as a "process in which those parties with a stake in the problem actively seek a mutually determined solution. They join forces, pool information, knock heads, construct alternative solutions, and forge an agreement."[15]

While not normally viewed as a "problem," a vision has certain commonalities with one. Certainly, many problems would arise if those affected by the proposed vision did not subscribe to its contents. In fact, in problem solving, a shared vision is an important consideration. Creating a shared vision allows stakeholders (both internal and external to the library) to discover common values. These shared values then enable participants to develop plans for future joint responsibility for common policy issues. By exploring where disagreements lie, stakeholders approaching the issues from different perspectives can find innovative solutions that transcend the limitations of their individual visions.[16]

However, visions do not just appear; they need to be created. Effective leaders look beyond today's distractions in order to meditate upon future possibilities. However, it is important to recognize that leadership can emerge from any point in the organization, and leadership implies a sense of vision: to see the continuity of the past in the present and of the present in the future. A successful vision statement will incorporate a vision of success that synthesizes the individual visions of the staff. How does this happen?

A shared vision involves a number of different steps, illustrated in figure 3-5, and may include

> *Assessing the library staff's present vision*   Customers, colleagues, and competitors can help the staff examine the present strategy and assess its viability and risks.

Figure 3-5 Two Scenarios about Creating a Vision

Steps in Creating a Vision	Scenario One	Scenario Two
Assess the library staff's present vision	The staff focuses on today and getting tasks done	The staff sees the library as increasingly important in a world of change
Reflect on customer service	Those who come to the library are served; telephone customers are served if time permits	The focus is on customer service; all products are designed to address customer needs and convenience
Reflect on the library's organizational framework	The library has a traditional, hierarchical organizational chart	Library management experiments with teams, matrix and orbit frameworks, and participative management
Confront relationship issues	Grievances must follow channels	Conflict is dealt with where it occurs, as informally as possible
Search for opportunities to initiate change, innovation, and growth	It is difficult to get each day's work finished; there is no time to be frivolous	Regular and routine planning sessions explore possibilities
Take risks and learn from mistakes	Mistakes are to be corrected; staff "plays it safe"	Mistakes are viewed as data for the next decision; risk-taking is rewarded
Develop and present the vision statement	The mission statement needs to be developed first	The vision-development process is shared by both staff and customers
Evaluate the vision	We'll "get around to it"	The vision is evaluated during the annual planning cycle
Update the vision	N/A	Environmental scanning identifies areas to be updated
Appreciate accomplishments	Someday . . .	Every achievement is cause for an impromptu "party"

SOURCE: Adapted from Dean Tjosvold, *Teamwork for Customers: Building Organizations That Take Pride in Serving* (San Francisco: Jossey-Bass, 1993), 72–3.

Reflecting on customer service   Collecting and analyzing information on service delivery, customer experiences, and customer opinions can suggest new directions.

Reflecting on the organizational framework   Staff can discuss the nature of productive teamwork and how it compares with the present organizational model.

Confronting relationship issues   Dealing directly with grievances and conflicts is essential to forging a shared vision.

Searching for opportunities to initiate change, innovation, and growth   Instead of waiting to respond to a crisis, the staff does "preventive maintenance" and participates in the management of the library.

Taking risks and learning from mistakes   In Western society, making a mistake is viewed as completely negative and to be avoided at all costs. The more-productive approach is to view each mistake as providing data to make the next decision better. Moreover, risk-taking is essential if progress is to be made.

Developing and presenting a short statement that outlines the vision   This effort is powerful and unifying, evoking images and metaphors in describing where the library wants to go.

Evaluating the vision   Staff can discuss the ways in which the library's code of ethics and value system do and do not support the strategy and organizational framework.

Updating the vision   The vision statement needs to be revised in light of internal and external changes. Customers' ideas and complaints, predictions from the field, and the claims of competitors should be taken into account.

Appreciating accomplishments   The staff should celebrate its capacity to change and reward the progress that is made.[17]

These steps are good benchmarks that can move the process along. Within each step, the following strategies can put energies in motion:

Brainstorm in group sessions as a way to identify windows of opportunity.

Use a "multiple futures" approach to assist participants in conceptualizing what the library "would like to be," "could be," and "is likely to be." Formulating alternative futures allows the freewheeling discussion necessary to escape the present.

Harness the emerging vision and make it real. For this to take place, the vision must be realistic, credible, and supported by a consensus of the stakeholders. Staff generally feel good about their participation in designing a future with a purpose and direction. Because they have established ownership, they are more likely to commit energies to making it happen.[18]

Realism and credibility are essential to true commitment. If an overly ambitious agenda is set, the organization can overreach what is possible. The tendency to overreach is frequently an outcome of an unwillingness to accept limits on what either the staff themselves or their libraries can do. The refusal to accept reality includes a habit of seriously underestimating the actual work involved in attaining a major objective. However, it is also possible to aim too low and be overly cautious. In this scenario, planners try to increase the chances of success and, in so doing, they prolong the decision process and run the risk of missing opportunities. The optimum course of action is to pursue a high order of organizational ambition while managing to keep objectives within reach. Knowing organizational limits while expressing grand dreams, such planners remain in touch with the gradual process of growth and evaluation that an organization must undertake to attain its vision.[19]

Mission and vision are like the two parts of the yin and yang symbol, complementary and essential to making a whole. The past informs the present, and the present serves as the headwater of the visionary stream of ideas and creativity. Figure 3-6 combines the yin/yang symbol with the mission/vision relationship.

A clear image of the future is essential for clarifying the gaps between the organization's current and future states. These gaps will form the basis for the transition strategy to be articulated in the goals and objectives of the planning process. A clear de-

Figure 3-6   The Mission/Vision Complement

Mission
• Building on past
• Informing the present

Vision
• Ideas
• Creativity
• Profiling the future

scription of the future state can also encourage dissatisfaction with the way things are, and the more dissatisfaction that emerges, the less resistance there will be to the change effort. This vision description needs to reach at least five years into the future and should describe the behaviors and conditions that will profile the future library.[20]

Not just any vision will do. The library's vision needs to be both strategic and far-reaching. The strategic element involves staying focused on customers and expressing in the vision how the library contributes to the community. The far-reaching aspects need to capture staff imagination and spirit. The vision is the staff's deepest expression of what is wanted. Putting a vision into words signifies staff dissatisfaction with what presently exists, exposes the future that staff hope to achieve, and forces staff to hold themselves accountable for behavior that is congruent with that vision. The vision states how the staff want to work with customers and with each other.[21]

However, a moment's digression into a reality check must acknowledge the very real tension between the advent of change and resistance to change. It is human nature to fear the unknown, and change is definitely the land of the unknown. Therefore, it is imperative that *everyone* to be affected by a decision must be involved in the making of that decision. If staff and customers are part of the process of change, they will be less fearful. The goal is to achieve a sense of ownership among all the stakeholders, both internal and external, and a shared pride in moving toward the desired vision.

In summary, the vision needs to be developed and communicated so that all stakeholders are invested in and excited about what is to come. We need to communicate hope and optimism, regardless of present conditions. Our language should embrace color and passion; emotionally charged words such as *greatness, service, integrity,* and *meaning* contribute to the vision's impact. Using metaphors and picture images can add clarity and enhance shared perceptions. Painting a specific picture of the future adds dimension and understanding.[22]

We can choose to seek out opportunities and possibilities, or we can choose to resist the changes. We can also just allow others to make the decisions as we drift along from day to day, month to month, year to year. These are serious choices. The library that will move proactively and vigorously into the next century will be staffed by individuals that make the choice to carve out an optimistic and customer-centered vision of the future while embracing all the challenges and risks that change will bring.

In chapter 4, our discussion shifts to the marketing audit and how it influences both mission and vision. Systems analysis will be used as the frame through which the audit data are examined.

THOUGHTS AND MUSINGS

Does my library have a mission statement? Could I tell a customer what that mission is?

Does my library have a vision statement? Could I share that vision with a customer?

What paradigm does my library embrace? Is it yesterday's, today's, or tomorrow's?

What might be the next paradigm that is coming?

How prepared is the library's staff to shift into the new paradigm? How prepared am I?

Notes

1. Weingand, Darlene E., *Customer Service Excellence: A Concise Guide for Librarians* (Chicago: American Library Assoc., 1997), 23.

2. Joel A. Barker, *Discovering the Future: The Business of Paradigms,* 2d ed. (Burnsville, Minn.: Infinity and Charthouse, 1989), video.

3. Barker.

4. Joel A. Barker, *Paradigm Pioneers*, Discovering the Future Series (Burnsville, Minn.: Charthouse, 1993), video.

5. Weingand, 70.

6. Barker, *Discovering the Future.*

7. Viktor E. Frankl, *Man's Search for Meaning* (New York: Pocket Books, 1959), 164–6.

8. Benjamin Singer, "The Future-Focused Role-Image," in *Learning for Tomorrow: The Role of the Future in Education,* ed. Alvin Toffler (New York: Random House, 1974), 19–32.

9. Andrew Campbell and Laura L. Nash, *A Sense of Mission* (New York: Addison-Wesley, 1990), chap. 3, quoted in Stephen R. Covey, A. Roger Merrill, and Rebecca R. Merrill, *First Things First* (New York: Simon & Schuster, 1994), 103.

10. Fred Polak, *The Image of the Future* (San Francisco: Jossey-Bass, 1972), quoted in Stephen R. Covey, A. Roger Merrill, and Rebecca R. Merrill, *First Things First* (New York: Simon & Schuster, 1994), 103.

11. Stephen R. Covey, A. Roger Merrill, and Rebecca R. Merrill, *First Things First* (New York: Simon & Schuster, 1994), 103–4.

12. Covey, Merrill, and Merrill, 105–6.

13. Covey, Merrill, and Merrill, 113.

14. Covey, Merrill, and Merrill, 116.

15. Barbara Gray, *Collaborating: Finding Common Ground for Multiparty Problems* (San Francisco: Jossey-Bass, 1989), xviii.

16. Jean Lipman-Blumen, *The Connective Edge: Leading in an Interdependent World* (San Francisco: Jossey-Bass, 1996), 169.

17. Dean Tjosvold, *Teamwork for Customers: Building Organizations That Take Pride in Serving* (San Francisco: Jossey-Bass, 1993), 72–3.

18. Donald E. Riggs, "Leadership Versus Management in Technical Services," in *Developing Leadership Skills: A Source Book for Librarians,* eds. Rosie L. Albritton and Thomas W. Shaughnessy (Englewood, Colo.: Libraries Unlimited, 1990), 229–30.

19. Robert E. Kaplan, *Beyond Ambition: How Driven Managers Can Lead Better and Live Better* (San Francisco: Jossey-Bass, 1991), 95–6.

20. Warren H. Schmidt and Jerome P. Finnigan, *The Race Without a Finish Line: America's Quest for Total Quality* (San Francisco: Jossey-Bass, 1992), 169–70.

21. Peter Block, *The Empowered Manager: Positive Political Skills at Work* (San Francisco: Jossey-Bass, 1989), 102–7.

22. Block, 121–23.

4

~~~~~~~

The Marketing Audit
Using Systems Analysis to Inform Market Research

Change is a constant in today's library environment. However, while creative and far-reaching mission and vision statements can chart present purpose and future direction, it is the marketing audit that will provide the data necessary to inform and reinforce this direction. In many ways, this is a typical "chicken and egg" scenario; it is debatable whether mission/vision precedes or follows the collection of data, and in most cases, the accurate answer may be "both." Certainly, whatever the library has in place as mission and vision statements must be subject to alteration once data have been collected and analyzed.

As a first step in initiating the marketing audit, it is important to recognize that the overall market is made up of many segments. *Market segmentation* is "the process of dividing customers into groups with unique characteristics and needs" and is central to an accurate definition of the market. All library customers (present and potential) can be divided into categories, each of which may require different kinds of service and support. The community that the library serves can be segmented by such factors as age, location, profession, department, and technical competence plus any other characteristic that may help the library to identify service requirements. Such an analysis leads to interrelated groups of customers, for the total community can be subdivided in multiple ways, with individuals and groups potentially sharing more than one attribute. The evolving mission statement is influenced by this market segmentation of the overall community, and the process lends substance and form to the development of goals, objectives, and action statements that follow.

The Library and Its Environments

The term *environment* is a complex concept composed of both internal and external components, each of which can be further subdivided. Internal and external environments need to be routinely assessed. Three terms are used fairly interchangeably to describe the process that analyzes the customer groups to be served: needs assessment, community analysis, and marketing audit. However, it is the marketing audit introduced in chapter 1 as the mnemonic device Prelude that is the umbrella term and encompasses the other terms. Specifically, all three terms can be compared in the following manner:

> *Needs assessment* addresses both customer-expressed (felt) and unexpressed needs, frequently using survey methodology or interview techniques to identify those needs. The needs of both internal and external environments should be researched.
>
> *Community analysis* also examines needs, but in the context of the whole community picture. Secondary data concerning demographic statistics and growth patterns lend structure to this process, and primary data collection fleshes out the identified parameters.
>
> *Marketing audit* covers both the assessment of customer needs and the attempt to understand community systems. Kotler defines the marketing audit as a "comprehensive, systematic, independent, and periodic examination of the library's total environment, objectives, strategies, ac-

tivities, and resources in order to determine problem areas and opportunities and to recommend a plan of action."[1] Almost every word in this definition could be expanded upon and should be considered carefully by the planning team, with particular attention to the process words *comprehensive, systematic, independent,* and *periodic.*

In addition to the external environment, the marketing audit analyzes the internal environment of the library—identifying strengths, limitations, and present practice—thereby including the entire environment in its examination. Furthermore, the audit develops an "environmental scan" (see chapter 5) that identifies trends and projections in both external and internal environments to develop contingency plans that will relate to alternative future scenarios.

Before a marketing audit of the library's several environments is initiated, certain fundamental points need to be considered.

As with the planning process, analysis of the environment is not an occasional activity. It must be ongoing so that trends and changing characteristics are detected as they bubble to the surface.

Environmental analysis needs to be a collaborative effort among library staff, policy board members, and representatives of the target markets in the community. The formation of this partnership establishes a foundation for working together to merge the library into the mainstream of community life. It is a learning opportunity for all who are involved and a good time for sharing perspectives and ideas.[2]

In addition, there may be surprises in the forthcoming data that will affect present perceptions of the realities of population demographics, perceived needs, and attitudes toward the library. New population groups may have emerged with specific needs for information and learning. Attitudes about what programs the library provides may call for a change in programming. These surprises may require adjustments in expectations, service emphases, and marketing strategies. It is vital that affected constituent groups, both internal and external to the library, be actively involved in the process and not be passive recipients of a final report.

As the marketing audit identifies those portions of the community that are presently unserved, a natural next step involves outreach efforts specifically targeted to those unserved groups. A corollary benefit of routine planning and analysis is the monitoring capability that can assess the effectiveness of such outreach efforts. There is a symbiotic relationship between environmental analysis and outreach that is clear in demonstrable outcomes.[3]

Finally, while the analysis can admirably sketch in general terms, the full palette of library service is reflected in the library's ability to respond to individual human beings with unique perceptions and needs.

Change is with us. The audit data can never be regarded as static or planning be regarded as a linear process. Even as the environment is being analyzed, the community is reacting to political, economic, and social influences. The marketing audit provides snapshots in time, nothing more. The task is simultaneously necessary and never completed. This statement is not meant to be discouraging. Rather, it points out the dynamic milieu in which the public library functions. The challenge is to seek out effective avenues for identifying and responding to community needs.[4]

In terms of the library's internal environment, analysis of the marketing audit data should provide a profile of strengths and limitations that includes the library's planning objectives, strategies, activities, and resources (human, fiscal, and physical). The profile should also outline the organizational climate, patterns of communication, organizational structure, and whatever elements of marketing practice are in place.

When analyzing the library's external environment, the following elements need to be considered:

> *Demographics* What are the attributes of the community, such as population, age, gender, educational background, income, employment, and so forth?

Geography   What constitutes the library's setting, land-scape, climate, transportation, and other physical attributes?

Sociology and Psychology   Who are the individuals and groups that compose the target markets? What are their preferences and biases? What are the social patterns? How do members of the community behave under different sets of circumstances or levels of stress? Can probable behavior be anticipated? Where is the power in the community, and how does it flow?

Economics   What is the overall fiscal health of the community? What major businesses/industries are in place or about to leave or enter the community? What is the current climate for business and growth?

Technology   What brands and types of hardware do members of the community presently own or plan to purchase in the next two years? What is the status of cable television, satellite dishes, and computer networks? What use does the business (including farm) community make of different technologies?

Politics   What is the library's relationship to funding sources, both public and private? How does political power relate to societal power? What kinds of lobbying/maneuvering have been done in the past? What worked, and what did not?

Culture   What intellectual and artistic activities are present in the community? Are there gaps that the library should attempt to fill? What cooperative ventures with other agencies could be proposed?

Competition   What agencies, businesses, vendors, organizations, or individuals provide similar products to those offered by the library? What areas of possible cooperation can be identified? Where do areas of duplication exist? (If the library cannot do it better, faster, or cheaper—and if the market cannot support both the library and the competitor[s] in this endeavor—then the library should consider reallocating its efforts into more unique and effective pursuits.)[5]

Figure 4-1   Examples of Data Elements in the
Library's Internal and External Environments

Data Element	Internal Environment	External Environment
Demographic	Staff size, organizational structure, distribution, scheduling	Population, age, income level, educational background, employment
Geographical	Location of access points	Setting, landscape, climate, transportation
Physical	State of building(s), equipment, collection	Condition of facilities of parent organization, identification of scheduled repairs and construction
Sociological	Intergroup and intragroup staff relationships, patterns of communication	Target markets, preferences and biases, social patterns, power flow
Psychological	Staff mental health, aspirations, motivation	Behavior under different circumstances and stress, anticipation of probable behavior
Economic	Staff salaries, staff benefits, size of library's budget, alternative funding in-hand	Overall fiscal health, types of businesses and industry, incoming/departing businesses, climate for growth
Technological	Presently available, anticipated, desirable	Types of hardware owned and anticipated, status of cable television, Internet access, etc.
Political	Unions (if applicable), organizational climate, planning objectives	Relationship to public and private funding sources, power flow, lobbying efforts
Cultural	Artistic programs such as art shows and concerts, decorations	Current artistic activities, opportunities for cooperative ventures, gaps to be filled
Competition	Between individuals, groups on staff	Agencies and businesses offering similar products, areas of present and possible duplication and cooperation

SOURCE: Adapted from Darlene E. Weingand, *Managing Today's Public Library: Blueprint for Change* (Englewood, Colo.: Libraries Unlimited, 1994), 20–1.

Figure 4-1 expands this conceptual frame and applies these data elements not only to the external environment but also to the internal environment.

Types of Market Research

Several roads into the external environment may be traveled. No single method is ideal, and each library must decide the most-appropriate strategy for assessing the local situation. The first stop on this journey is secondary-source data—those pieces of information that have already been collected by other organizations or units. It is important to not "reinvent the wheel," and data that are already available should be used to the fullest extent possible.

Once this avenue has been exhausted and the planning team has identified gaps in information that need to be addressed, it is both timely and appropriate to consider one or more options for primary-data collection—going directly to the community to gather data. Sampling methodology is generally used to establish an N (number to be surveyed) of reasonable size. Many basic books of statistics provide instruction on sampling procedures and a table of random numbers to use as a base. Research has repeatedly affirmed the use of sampling procedures (instead of surveying entire populations). The results of sampling stand up very well and save the library a good deal of effort and cost.

One of the most-often-used methods for collecting primary data is the questionnaire/survey. However, the questionnaire (or interview schedule) is only as useful as the questions it asks. Before the questionnaire is written, the library administration must determine what it wants to know. Seek only data required to aid in decision making; strenuously avoid the temptation to throw in questions because "it would be interesting to know."

No one is born knowing how to write a questionnaire. Therefore, unless someone on the library staff has had training in this skill, enlist a knowledgeable member of the community to assist in the questionnaire design. Such an individual might be found in local businesses or in high school or college/university departments such as business, education, or statistics.

The next step is to pretest the questionnaire with a small group of volunteers who share characteristics with the target sample. This pretest will pinpoint ambiguous statements and items that are unclear. The revised questionnaire is then ready to use. There are several approaches to surveying the individuals identified in the sample, including telephone survey, mail survey, interview, focus group, and community meeting.

Telephone Survey

The telephone survey is one of the easiest methods to use. Once a sampling frame is established, use the local telephone book as the source of names to call. However, this source imposes a bias that must be acknowledged because unlisted numbers are not part of the population to be sampled. A more valid method involves using the computer to randomly generate telephone numbers; many colleges or universities have research labs that are equipped to provide this service.

Those individuals who will be placing the calls must be trained in interview techniques. Depending on the design of the sample frame, the calls may be assigned different categories such as head of household, teenager, adult female, adult male, etc. If the completed call does not yield a person to be interviewed from the appropriate category, the caller must move on to the next telephone number. In addition, interview etiquette suggests that the opening phrase be something like, "This is the XYZ Library, and we are conducting a brief survey of our community. This will take approximately ten minutes of your time. Is this a good time to talk, or shall I call back later?" If the interview can proceed, the person to be surveyed must be asked the same questions in the same order as every other person called.

Mail Survey

The mail survey differs from the telephone survey in the language used and the structure of the responses. The questions are a bit more formal, since there is no opportunity for questioning the customer's intent—which is possible during the one-on-one exchange of the telephone interview. This method has the poorest return rate (30 to 50 percent). A self-addressed, stamped envelope must be enclosed to ensure any return rate of substance.

Interview

Another approach entirely is the in-person interview of library users (in the library), general community (in person, outside the library), or both. The interview strategies of the telephone survey also apply to the face-to-face interview situation.

This method is staff time-intensive in that a designated and trained staff member (paid or unpaid) conducts each in-depth interview, but the opportunity for individualized information gathering can have unique benefits. Many attitudes and perceptions may emerge that would not have surfaced in a simple questionnaire format.

Focus Group

An expansion of the interview is the focus group. A trained facilitator gathers a small group of invited participants (with shared knowledge, experience, or interest in predetermined areas) to explore needs and options. No interview schedule of questions is prepared; rather, the facilitator begins with broad, general questions and leads the group to focus more and more tightly on specifics as the exercise progresses. Because it is possible to probe more deeply, this method can be extremely helpful when charting future directions and gathering data for decision making.

Community Meeting

Although commonly used to encourage community involvement, the community meeting is not suggested as a means to reach the indifferent or the nonuser. Participants in such a meeting or hearing should be regarded as interested parties because they have made the effort to attend. Once participants have assembled, the following procedure may be used to structure the event:

> *Introductions* This opening provides for a sharing of personal information among members of the group/audience (depending on size) that may include names, addresses, occupations, or other information that may be of significance or interest in a particular community.
>
> *Brainstorming* During brainstorming the participants propose ideas in rapid succession with no judgment or

evaluation of their merit. Ideas may incorporate citizen concerns, needs, wishes, hopes, and dreams for library service and operation. A designated recorder lists all ideas as they occur on large flip charts, attaching completed sheets to the walls around the room with masking tape. Formal nominal group methodology can be a very useful structure for this stage. The nominal group technique enables all good ideas to be presented, as it levels the playing field between the very vocal and the more reticent team members. All team members are instructed to silently write down all their ideas regarding a designated topic. When all ideas have been written down, each team member (one at a time) states one idea—which is then written on a flip chart. Each team member is polled in turn and the circuit is continued until all ideas have been placed on the flip chart and numbered. No judgments as to the merits of an idea are allowed at this point. Once all ideas are collected, the team members are instructed to "choose their favorite five." Once again, the team is polled, and hash marks are placed next to each selected idea. The top "vote-getting" ideas are to be considered first by the team; however, all ideas are retained for future discussions.[6]

Social hour   Social hour provides an opportunity for participants to discuss proposed ideas informally over coffee. During this time, the recorder arranges (and recopies where necessary) the suggestions into logical categories—funding, hours of service, service to target markets, use of technology, etc.

Discussion   The discussion period is a collective sharing of ideas and opinions by the reassembled group.

Ranking   In this final step the group, either together through discussion or independently on paper, ranks the suggestions in priority order. (A "quick and dirty" method is for each person to select their "favorite five" from each category.) The recorder tallies all responses and highlights the top vote-getters. (Note: In communities where interactive cable TV or community computer bulletin boards are available, an alternative possibility for this step would be to allow citizens to provide input electronically. This would add depth to the exercise and encourage wider participation.)

A combination of these methods may be effective. The individual library staff decides what seems both reasonable and appropriate to the local situation. Certainly, the more input that can be gathered, the more community involvement has taken place and there will be a heightened sense of ownership among community members.

In summary, to analyze the library's environments, assets, and limitations, a four-step process is indicated:

1. Determine what data elements will be covered. Consider depth of coverage, amount and type of resources available to conduct the audit, and planning team/staff expectations of outcomes.

2. Develop procedures for collecting data and monitoring the process.

3. Collect and analyze the data. Use secondary sources first and supplement with primary-source data collection where gaps are identified.

4. Prepare reports and presentations of the results. Use both written and oral reports, incorporating summaries and graphics.[7]

Futures Strategy: Systems Analysis

The simplest conceptualization of an entity defined by its organizational invariance is that of a system. A system in this definition is a collection of parts conserving some identifiable set of (internal) relations, with the summed relations (that is, the system itself) conserving some identifiable set of (external) relations to other entities (systems).[8]

In library terms, the library is a collection of parts (staff, collection, services, programs, and physical facilities) that relate to each other internally, yet also relate as a whole to other entities/systems in the external environment. Such external systems could include the city/town, university campus, school, or corporation. Still other systems would consist of the library's multiple segmented markets and customer groups.

Figure 4-2 Comparison of System Hierarchies

*Individual Needs**

Aesthetic needs
(perceiving beauty, order)

Cognitive needs
(relations, comprehending order)

Self-actualization need
(fulfilling potential)

Esteem needs
(respect of others)

Belongingness/love needs
(family, social group)

Safety needs
(protection, job security)

Physiological needs
(food, air, water)

Library Needs

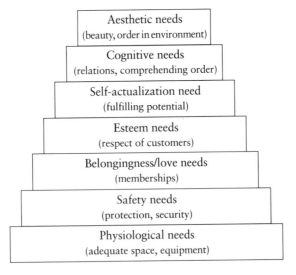

Aesthetic needs
(beauty, order in environment)

Cognitive needs
(relations, comprehending order)

Self-actualization need
(fulfilling potential)

Esteem needs
(respect of customers)

Belongingness/love needs
(memberships)

Safety needs
(protection, security)

Physiological needs
(adequate space, equipment)

*SOURCE: Adapted from Abraham H. Maslow, *Motivation and Personality* (New York: Harper and Row, 1970).

Graphically, the entire concept could be drawn as circles within circles.

Brought down to the level of the individual, a human being is also an open system that interacts with the environment and, ultimately, with society. Maslow, Piaget, Bruner, and Koestler have developed hierarchies that describe those system interactions. Figure 4-2 illustrates an inclusive hierarchy of the individual in the top pyramid and a corresponding interpretation of the library's system hierarchy in the bottom pyramid. The examples given in figure 4-2 are representative only, and many more examples (such as funding level, autonomy, etc.) could have been listed. The meaning to be grasped here is that the library, like the individual, has levels of needs within an overall system. It is to this overall system that the interpretation of marketing audit data must relate.

The application of systems analysis to marketing and planning involves the choice of policies and the design of action programs to carry out the plan. Further, if these actions are to be practical and useful rather than just an exercise of the imagination, available resources and expected payoffs must be taken into consideration.[9] In other words, the entire system of the library and its interactions with various environments must be part of the analysis process, and decisions must be made that are based on a careful appraisal of the library's functions and cost-effectiveness. When the lens through which decision makers look is focused on the complete system rather than on a fragment, the quality of those decisions is enhanced. Questions to be addressed include systems costs, systems benefits, and representative scenarios.

Systems Costs

For each decision, what are the nonmonetary social costs that must be considered? How do these costs relate to identified monetary costs?

How can future costs be estimated with reliability? How should future costs be compared with present costs?

How should expenditures be compared with investments?

Since future costs depend in part on today's realities, can a cross-impact model be designed in which the impacts of events and trend changes on costs are systematically analyzed? (For further discussion, see chapter 7.)

Systems Benefits

Given a library product for the future of which plans are to be made, what is an appropriate set of social or other indicators by which a future condition of that product can be described and different future conditions can be compared?

What are the customer groups whose needs/wants regarding the future condition of that product must be considered?

What rational methods are there for assigning weights to these different groups?

What dimensions of satisfaction relative to the future condition of this product can be identified and measured?

How does this future product relate to the library's goals and objectives?

Can the cross-impact model be extended to include benefit cross impacts (as well as costs) or a second model be developed? (Both diminished or enhanced benefits should be reflected in such a model.)

Representative Scenarios

Considering the multiple possible scenarios of the future, is it possible to identify a small, manageable set of "representative" scenarios for planning purposes? (See chapter 6 for further discussion on scenario building.)

Can the planning team then focus decision making based on the contingencies depicted in the representative scenarios—and still be reasonably confident that these decisions could be generalized to unanticipated scenarios?[10]

If the data from the marketing audit is approached from a systems perspective and also incorporates futurist thinking, the data become more dynamic and less static. However, the temptation to quantify everything in an objective frame must be resisted. Systems analysis in the library setting more successfully resides in philosophy than in statistics. Its primary contribution lies in developing a vision of the library within larger and larger circles of influence and activity.

The next chapter takes a closer look at environmental scanning with particular emphasis on the Delphi Method as a means for gathering data.

THOUGHTS AND MUSINGS

Has my library ever done a marketing audit? When was the last time? Is it time to do another?

In previous marketing audits, did we omit any important parts?

In terms of the internal environment, what are my library's strengths and limitations?

What are the attributes of the external environment within which my library operates?

As we begin our marketing audit, what secondary sources are available in our community? in the library? What agencies in my community can provide data regarding future trends?

What method(s) should we use to gather primary data?

Notes

1. Philip Kotler, *Marketing for Nonprofit Organizations* (Englewood Cliffs, N.J.: Prentice-Hall, 1982), 185.
2. Darlene E. Weingand, *Managing Today's Public Library: Blueprint for Change* (Englewood, Colo.: Libraries Unlimited, 1994), 21–2.
3. Weingand, 22.
4. Weingand, 22.
5. Weingand, 20–1.
6. Darlene E. Weingand, *Customer Service Excellence: A Concise Guide for Librarians* (Chicago: ALA, 1997), 53.
7. Weingand, *Managing Today's Public Library,* 22–3.
8. Ervin Laszlo, *A Strategy for the Future: The Systems Approach to World Order* (New York: George Braziller, 1974), 17–18.
9. Olaf Helmer, "The Research Tasks before Us," in *Handbook of Futures Research,* ed. Jib Fowles (Westport, Conn.: Greenwood, 1978), 773.
10. Helmer, 773.

5

Making a
Futures Screen
Using the
Delphi Method

Although the marketing audit provides an essential baseline for identifying customer needs, it cannot be regarded as more than a snapshot in time. The audit examines the present: those current resources, opportunities, and limitations that create the boundaries of possibility. However, there is more that must be learned if the library is to effectively serve the community. This additional intelligence resides in the "what might be" rather than in the "what is."

This chapter uses the term *futures screen*, which is a metaphoric way of suggesting that all of the components of the marketing/planning process should be sifted through a screen of alternative futures, allowing ideas meriting further development to pass through and removing the remainder from further immediate consideration. For the purposes of this chapter, the screening process will be defined as "environmental scanning."

What Is an Environmental Scan?

Environmental scanning relates to the external environment: the world and events outside the library. What goes on in this external environment—not only today but, more specifically, projected into tomorrow—can have reverberating effects on what happens to the library internally. The purpose of environmental scanning is to gain information regarding trends, events, and issues that may produce impacts upon library operations. It is intended to reduce uncertainty, surprise, and ambiguity by increasing our awareness of the world around us in focused ways. Areas of concern to be targeted include economic fluctuations, technological advancements, social change, and legislative/regulatory impacts.[1]

Why is environmental scanning important? Today's library tries to stay afloat in "permanent white water," with change affecting operations on a daily basis. Environmental scanning is one way to bring some degree of order to this chaos and to expose the library to competitive intelligence about the world outside its walls. It is also an opportunity for staff to become proactive and engage in creative problem solving regarding the library's future activities.

From an organizational perspective, the library itself becomes energized and more in tune with its community through environmental scanning. Staff development is also enhanced through participation in the scanning process because employees help shape how the library functions and how it addresses the future. Such essential skills as critical thinking, writing, and speaking are practiced as part of the scan, and team building can be an unanticipated benefit.

Using the Environmental Scan in Library Planning/Marketing

There are four steps that form the typical environmental scan as applied in the library context:

1. The external environment is monitored for emerging issues, trends, or developments that may pose an opportu-

nity or threat to the library. During the gathering of data in a marketing audit, current trends and projections are gathered. These trends can be identified through the secondary data routinely collected by county planning commissions, corporate marketing units, and so forth. In addition, between formal marketing audits, library staff need to be alert to changing conditions and factor what they learn into the overall marketing/planning process.

2. The identified trends, issues, or developments are evaluated and ranked according to importance and potential for impact on the community and on library services.

3. A determination is made regarding how and when to apply this information to the marketing/planning process and make process adjustments.

4. Each trend, issue, or development is then reassessed for inclusion in additional or continued scanning efforts.[2]

To accomplish these four steps, resources are needed. Documents—such as newspapers, journals, government publications, the Internet, and other "hard copy" and electronic materials—form the object of the scan, but the biggest resource requirement is that of people. Staff members, whether paid or unpaid (volunteer), are needed to do the actual scanning, coordinate the effort, and disseminate the results. It is the human mind that has the capacity to scan for data and organize the outcome in a meaningful way. Identifying data, setting priorities, and relating data to library planning are critical staff responsibilities.

The environmental scan places considerable emphasis on securing all available data on what "might be" in the next five years (and beyond). In practical terms, objectives can then be developed to reflect that informed projection. The development of parallel sets of contingency objectives creates working documents that can be referred to as conditions change. These sets of alternative objectives provide thoughtfully considered decisions regarding foreseen—but not yet real—scenarios. Moreover, the very existence of alternative objectives maintains the library in a proactive state and, no matter how severe a crisis, forestalls the potential waste of a reactive response.

Alternative sets of objectives are written so that the library continues to work toward established goals regardless of possible community changes. These three sets of objectives for each goal address the following situations:

- conditions (economic, societal, political, etc.) remain similar to the present
- conditions change markedly in a positive direction
- conditions change markedly in a negative direction

In the case of funding alone, these three vastly different scenario possibilities might prompt objectives that would be very different. Further, time is a significant variable here, as projections for one year into the future can be more detailed and probable than projections for five years. Yet, both must be made —both one- and five-year forecasts must be constructed if effective proactive planning is to occur.

However, too often, staff members believe themselves to be too busy to engage in a scan or are convinced that they already know what is important in serving the community. Four questions can easily dispel these myths:

1. Do we really understand our environment—or is the (library) suffering from internal information overload, white noise from the world outside, and too little information of the "right" kind? (Are we buried under a blizzard of data and information that we do not understand?)
2. Are we missing valuable opportunities because we do not have timely and useful information about what is going on "out there"?
3. Is our (library) fully equipped and [are] our employees fully skilled to deal with changing environments and ensure our success—now and in the future?
4. Are we in danger of hitting icebergs?[3]

A yes answer to any of these questions is definite evidence that environmental scanning will be useful to the library.

Futures Strategy: The Delphi Method

One possible futures research strategy for scanning the environment and identifying trends is the Delphi Method. Characterized as a method for structuring a group communication process so that the process is effective in allowing a group of individuals, as a whole, to deal with a complex problem, the Delphi experiment in the use of group opinion has extended from the early 1950s.[4] The unique properties of the Delphi Method have recognized value in terms of both usefulness and exploration of rational alternative futures.

History and Development

The Delphi Method was developed by the RAND Corporation in conjunction with defense research. "Project Delphi" was the name given to an Air Force-sponsored RAND Corporation study in the early 1950s concerning the use of expert opinion, with an eye toward achieving reliable consensus by a group of experts. In 1953 Norman C. Dalkey and Olaf Helmer introduced a new technique into the process: iteration with controlled feedback. The set of procedures that have subsequently evolved has been named *Delphi*, although there is no intended connection to the ancient Greek oracle.

In 1959 Helmer and RAND researcher Nicholas Rescher published "The Epistemology of the Inexact Sciences," a document that gave a philosophical base to forecasting. The paper argued that "in fields that have not yet developed to the point of having scientific laws, the testimony of experts is permissible."[5]

The Delphi procedures increased in general interest with the publication of Gordon and Helmer's study of forecasting technological events.[6] The aim of this study was to assess the direction of long-range trends (10 to 50 years), with special emphasis on science and technology and their probable effects. The study coincided with a surge of interest in long-range forecasting and in the systematic use of expert opinion.[7]

In the spring of 1968, a series of experiments were conducted at RAND to evaluate the procedures and to explore the nature of the information processes occurring during Delphi interaction. Upperclass and graduate students were used as subjects and general information from almanacs as subject matter. Two group methods were tested: face-to-face discussion and controlled-feedback interaction. Findings indicated that face-to-face discussion tended to result in less-accurate group forecasting estimates, while anonymous controlled feedback resulted in more-accurate estimates.[8] These experiments put the Delphi techniques in a more-secure methodological position.

After 1969 there was a marked increase in applications of the Delphi procedures by industry for forecasting technological developments and by organizations for consideration of policy decisions. From the United States, the Delphi Method has spread to Western and Eastern Europe and the Far East. It has found its way into government, industry, and academe. It responds to a demand for improved communications among groups that are either too large or too geographically dispersed to be satisfied by other techniques.[9] Consequently, it becomes a valuable research tool for use in environmental scanning.

Properties

The intuitive forecasting technique of the Delphi Method is based on the opinions and judgments of experts in a designated field. The use of experts recognizes their importance in the decision-making process and the fact that they are in a position to influence future policy. The Delphi procedures have three general features:

1. *Anonymity* Opinions of members of the group are obtained by formal questionnaire.

2. *Iteration and controlled feedback* Interaction is effected by a systematic exercise conducted in several iterations with carefully controlled feedback between rounds.

3. *Statistical group response* The group opinion is defined as an appropriate aggregate of individual opinions on the final round.

These features were designed to minimize the bias produced by dominant individuals, group pressure, and irrelevant communications.[10] A statistical index of some type was needed to report representative group opinion, and the median was selected as a measure of central tendency. Subsequently, the interquartile range was also calculated on the responses, and participants who fell outside this range were invited to either change their answer or provide an explanation for their position.

The Delphi Method has a different research epistemology than standard survey techniques and focuses on the gathering and generating of cultural information in a mode similar to a conference by mail. In the Delphi Method, problem solving is approached through application of group intuitive expertise. Panelists are required to respond individually and anonymously to several administrations of the same questionnaire statements. Between these rounds, statistical feedback concerning both individual and group responses is provided to each panelist. Throughout the process participants have an opportunity to change responses.

Numerous modifications have been made to the conventional Delphi Method, including the

> distinction between questions of likelihood of occurrence and desirability
>
> use of various feedback procedures for reporting group responses, including the feedback of reasons for responses
>
> use of increased ranges of criteria against which participants are required to judge events such as likely consequences, projected interventions, and the desirability of the event (or policy)
>
> use of a number of subpopulations of respondents rather than a single population
>
> collection of judgments of timing for future events as a period between earliest and latest dates rather than as a single date
>
> use of self-appraisal of expertness by respondents to weight item responses to improve reliability[11]

An additional modification is the potential use of the computer to carry out the calculation of group results in "real time." While this type of electronic tabulation has the advantage of eliminating the time lag inherent in the paper-and-pencil

Delphi, respondents would have significantly less time for consideration of individual issues.

General Applications

The Delphi Method has been used in futures research as a

> forecasting probe useful for predicting alternative futures in addition to those indicated by current trends
>
> preference probe that attempts to obtain information that is essentially about the participants themselves
>
> strategy probe useful for advising on selection of a strategy to meet a given set of objectives from a number of alternatives
>
> probe of perceptions of a current situation to collect data from which possible needs can be inferred
>
> pedagogical tool to teach people to think (about selected issues) [12]

The Delphi Method in Practice

The Delphi Method is a highly labor-intensive research technique. The following five steps form a framework for conducting a Delphi study.

1. *Select the Delphi panel.*   Comprising multiple iterations and controlled feedback, the Delphi Method is a shared experience among the panelists. The method does not select a random sample; it invites participants who share common characteristics. Identify up to five interest groups as having a potential impact on the future of your library. Some examples might be funders (public and private, including politicians), library users, library practitioners, and technologists. Criteria for selection of individuals within these groups could include professional affiliations, professional-association involvement, geographical distribution, job description, and policy-making capability.

The validity and reliability of the Delphi study are dependent upon the characteristics of the experts used as panel members. These characteristics include

Representativeness of the panel   A sufficient number of panelists have been gathered to ensure that the outcome accurately represents thinking in a field.

Appropriateness and competence of the panel   Each panel member has been carefully and appropriately chosen and has the competence/knowledge to make the judgments required.

Commitment of the panel   Panel members agree to give carefully considered judgments to the questionnaire iterations—a significant pledge of time.

Clarity of the questionnaire   The questionnaire will have been pretested so that panelists understand the questionnaire items.

Independence of responses   The anonymity attribute of the Delphi Method ensures that responses will not be affected by the pressures or personality impacts of a convened group.[13]

Personally invite to participate a final panel of up to 50 persons representing the interest groups (approximately 10 to 15 panelists per group). It is important to remember that the Delphi Method is invitational and not a random sample. Clearly communicate, both verbally and in writing, the importance of the study and the time required. Secure from each panelist a signed form or postcard indicating the panelist's understanding of the project and agreement to participate.

2. **Round 0.**   No more than four or five Delphi Rounds need be prepared. The opening round, 0, uses an open-ended questionnaire and asks the panel to respond with *change statements* reflecting the external and internal environmental issues categories that are provided to them. The initial question that the panel considers may be similar to that given in figure 5-1.

Sample issues categories are shown in figure 5-2. Provide sufficient space (at least two inches) after each category so that panel members have ample room to write in their change statements.

3. **Round 1.**   The responses received from Round 0 are then synthesized into a list of change statements that form the basis for Round 1. Responses are sorted into piles, with responses reflecting similar views clustered together. Clustered responses are

Figure 5-1   Sample Round 0 Introductory Question

Delphi Round 0 Question

There are forces at work that may induce changes in society and in the XXX Library within the next 20 years. On this questionnaire, please consider and respond to the following:

1. List changes in each of the following categories (see figure 5-2)
2. That will likely occur in this state
3. By the year 2020

Figure 5-2   Sample Round 0 Categories

Environment	*Change Category*	*Response Examples*
External	Social system changes, including socialization, institutions, roles, stratification	Rising level of education, fiscal constraints
External	Changes in customers	Computer literate, more older adults
External	Changes in social aspirations	Simplified life style focus on environment
External	New technology	Smaller computers, telecommunications
Internal	Changes in library functions and services	Computerized reserves, delivery to home/office
Internal	Changes in library structure in the community	Partnerships with other agencies, local access to the Internet
Internal	Changes in library administration	Program budgeting, style of management
Internal	Changes in professional skills	Staffing levels, staff development
?????	The X factor	(Any event/change that does not fit into the above categories)

then synthesized wherever possible in the process of creating the change statements for Round 1. While it is tempting to create many change statements from the panelist responses, use restraint. It will be easier on both panelists and the researcher if the number of statements can be kept under 100. (A mantra of "brief is beautiful" could be chanted!) In the sample of Round 1 given in figure 5-3, only one change statement is illustrated. In Round 1, four questions are asked concerning each change statement:

- likelihood/probability
- confidence in one's response
- date of the change
- desirability

4. *Round 2.*   In processing Round 1 and preparing Round 2, the median and interquartile range are computed from the Round 1 responses and marked on photocopies of Round 1 for return to the panel along with a compilation of panelists' comments.

In Round 2, the form provided to the panel begins with a space for comment where panelists who had original responses falling outside the marked interquartile range are invited to state the reason(s) for their positions—or change their original response(s). (It can be helpful to put a red star by the "out-of-range" responses to alert panelists that they must either justify their position or revise their response[s] to fall within the interquartile range.)

In Round 2, two additional questions are asked regarding each change statement—importance and impact—followed by a final comment space for the panelists to share additional perceptions. (See figure 5-4.)

5. *Round 3.*   In Round 3, the Round 2 responses are processed in similar fashion to Round 1. In addition, the median and interquartile range are recomputed for prior questions 1–4 to reflect changes of opinion. This revised feedback is marked on each panelist's photocopy. The first column in Round 3 again requests panelist rationale for being outside the interquartile range.

Figure 5-3   Example of One Change Statement for Round 1

Change Statement	Question 1 *What is the likelihood/ probability that the change will occur?*	Question 2 *What confidence do you have in your judgment concerning the probability of this particular change?*	Question 3 *If you believe this change will occur, by when will it occur?*	Question 4 *Should this change occur?*
	1 - Certain 2 - Probable 3 - Uncertain 4 - Not probable 5 - Impossible	1 - Highest confidence 2 - High confidence 3 - Uncertain 4 - Low confidence 5 - Lowest confidence	1 - 2005 2 - 2010 3 - 2015 4 - 2020 5 - 2025	1 - Yes, definitely 2 - Yes, probably 3 - Uncertain 4 - Probably not 5 - Absolutely not
Rapid change and constant crisis avoidance will require continual education updating and learning of coping skills	1 2 3 4 5	1 2 3 4 5	1 2 3 4 5	1 2 3 4 5

Figure 5-4 Example of One Change Statement for Round 2

Change Statement	Comment	Question 5	Question 6	Comment
	Please state your reason(s) for your response(s) if starred in red.	What is the importance of each change statement to libraries? Rate it accordingly.	If this change occurs, what will be its impact?	Additional perceptions you wish to share with the panel
		1 - Highest priority 2 - High priority 3 - Uncertain 4 - Low priority 5 - Lowest priority	1 - Very great 2 - Considerable 3 - Moderate 4 - Little 5 - None	
Rapid change and constant crisis avoidance will require continual education updating and learning of coping skills		1 2 3 4 5	1 2 3 4 5	

Then one additional question is added, addressing promotion by constituency groups. Finally, a comment space is provided for panelist explanation of any changes that they have made throughout the Delphi experience. (See figure 5-5 for an example of Round 3.)

When Round 3 is returned to the panel, the following several enclosures can be appended:

- the "Minority Report" representing the rationale of those panelists holding positions outside the interquartile range
- optional comments
- an evaluation form
- a brief demographics questionnaire

In summary, environmental scanning is essential to good planning, and the Delphi Method works well as a means to gather important, future-related information. It provides a way to collect data from a large number of persons without the restrictions of geography or scheduling. Although time-intensive, it is straightforward in its administration and less expensive than convening a group of similar size. Its unique attributes of anonymity, iteration, and controlled feedback produce a more-thoughtful and accurate result than many other possible techniques.

Once community input has been collected, it is time to design library products that will relate to the needs that have been identified. Chapter 6 takes a close look at the library's products and explores using the futures strategy of scenario building to help in identifying future products.

Figure 5-5 Example of One Change Statement for Round 3

Change Statement	Comment	Question 7	Comment
	Please state your reason(s) for your response(s) if starred in red.	Which one of the following customer groups will most promote and which one will most hinder this change? (Please *circle* the letter of the "promote" response and place an "X" over the "hinder" response.)	If you have changed your response at any point in this Delphi, please indicate your reason(s) opposite the appropriate change statement.
		1 - U.S. Congress	
		2 - State legislature	
		3 - City/county government	
		4 - Library users	
		5 - Library workers (etc.)	
		6 - Other (specify)	
		1	
		2	
		3	
		4	
		5	
		6	
Rapid change and constant crisis avoidance will require continual education updating and learning of coping skills			

THOUGHTS AND MUSINGS

Has my library ever done an environmental scan? When and how?

How accurate was the information that was gathered? Should other scanning processes be tried?

Would a Delphi study be useful in forecasting my community's future?

What interest groups would be appropriate from which to invite panelists?

Who might be asked to serve as representatives of each of these interest groups?

Who in the library or in the community might help with administration of the study?

Notes

1. George Kubik, "Future Views: External Environmental Scanning," *Future Trends* 28, no. 2 (Mar./Apr. 1997): 1.

2. Kubik, 1.

3. Kubik, 1.

4. Harold A. Linstone and Murray Turoff, eds., *The Delphi Method: Techniques and Applications* (Reading, Mass.: Addison-Wesley, 1975), 3.

5. Otto Helmer and Nicholas Rescher, "The Epistemology of the Inexact Sciences," *Management Sciences* 6, no. 1 (1959), as quoted in Edward Cornish, *The Study of the Future: An Introduction to the Art and Science of Understanding and Shaping Tomorrow's World* (Washington, D.C.: World Future Society, 1977), 85.

6. R. J. Gordon and O. Helmer, "Report on a Long-Range Forecasting Study" (Paper #P-2982) (Santa Monica, Calif.: RAND Corp., Sept. 1964).

7. N. C. Dalkey, "The Delphi Method: An Experimental Study of Group Opinion" (Memoranda #RM-5888-PR) (Santa Monica, Calif.: RAND Corp., June 1969), 15.

8. Dalkey, v–vi.

9. Linstone and Turoff, 11.

10. Dalkey, v.

11. B. McGaw, R. K. Browne, and P. Rees, "Delphi in Education: Review and Assessment," *Australian Journal of Education,* 20 (Mar. 1976): 60.

12. Stephen P. Hencley and James R. Yates, eds., *Futurism in Education* (Berkeley, Calif.: McCutchan, 1974), 99–102.

13. Richard Weatherman and Karen Swenson, "Delphi Technique," in *Futurism in Education: Methodologies,* eds. Stephen P. Hencley and James R. Yates (Berkeley, Calif.: McCutchan, 1974), 103.

6

❦

Using Scenarios
Identifying Future Products

The process of designing library products for a changing environment, which incorporates both planning and marketing elements, is more than a sum of its parts. When the intent of the effort is the marriage of excellent products with customer needs and a proactive, future-oriented attitude, the outcome has every probability of achieving a partnership of mutual benefit between the library and the community. It is to this end that designing for change aspires.

The Concept of Product

As explained in chapter 1, the concept of Product has been transferred from the for-profit sector to include items or services provided in the nonprofit sector as well. Following are two ways to identify and define Product as it applies to libraries.

Product Mix, Product Line, and Product Item

The library's products can be viewed within the triple construct of product mix, product line, and product item. Figure 6-1 illustrates how these three concepts relate to each other. This arrangement puts the various library products into context: individual product items collected into product lines that express commonality of purpose and product lines that form the overall mix of products offered by the library to the community.

Once the concept of product is accepted relative to library operations, the relationship to what the library offers becomes more than an analogy. The library provides a range of products/services to its community, including its collection, reference/information services, hours during which there is access to the collection and professional expertise, bibliographic instruction and other programming, and so forth. Some of the library's products are traditional and have been in existence for many years. Other products have been developed more recently, such as online searching, microcomputers for in-library use, and databases on CD-ROM, to name a few. The library's product mix is (or should be) continually changing in response to evolving customer and community needs. Since we are living in a world in which evolution is so fast-paced that it approaches revolution, the staff must continually monitor the environment for product ideas and alterations.

Product Expansion and Contraction

Especially in a time of rapid change, it is important that library managers and staff continually assess and reassess the products

Figure 6-1   The Product Mix

Product Line	Product Items
Collection	Books, videos, periodicals, films, phonodiscs, CDs, audio cassettes, art prints, etc.
Services	Circulation, interlibrary loan, online searches, reference service, delivery service
Programs	Bibliographic instruction, film series, literacy tutoring, art shows

currently being offered in the light of community needs, developing technologies, and societal shifts. Too often, the library's products remain the same, with additions during times when money is available and little movement when funding is tight. However, there may be no real analysis of product timeliness and effectiveness. Figure 6-2 shows some examples of product expansion and contraction. Note that individual products can be expanded as well; for example, 200 videos can be expanded to 400 or contracted to 100.

In nature, organisms are born, grow and mature, decline, and pass on. This must also happen to products. There is a time for a product to emerge; it will develop and enjoy a peak time; there will be an inevitable decline due to changing conditions; and finally, there must come a time when it is phased out. In libraries, this life cycle may be interrupted during the decline phase because of staff reluctance to part with traditional services, and products may "hang on" long past the point of real effectiveness.

Figure 6-2   Examples of Product Expansion and Contraction

Product Line	*Present Product Items*	*Expansion of Product Line*	*Contraction of Product Line*
Collection	Books, videos, periodicals, audio cassettes, phonodiscs, etc.	Computer programs, video discs	Elimination of phonodiscs
Services	Circulation, interlibrary loan, online searches, homebound service, etc.	Direct-to-office delivery system	Elimination of homebound service
Programs	Bibliographic instruction, story hours, film series, art shows, etc.	Income tax assistance	Elimination of film series

Expansion of Product Mix:
Add food service and gift shop

Contraction of Product Mix:
Eliminate programs

When this happens, the creativity and energy of new product development can be forestalled.

The "Apple" Concept of Product

Philip Kotler, in *Marketing for Nonprofit Organizations,* describes product with core, tangible, and augmented product aspects.[1] An apple can be used as a visual symbol of this concept. (See figure 6-3.) Every product has a core product, which is the aspect of product that normally defines the essence of the product. For example, when a customer interacts with the library while seeking to learn about Alaska before taking a cruise, the core product is information. The tangible product—the form in which the core product is presented and, in the apple metaphor,

Figure 6-3   The "Apple" Concept of Product

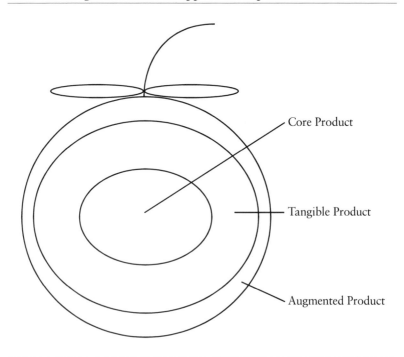

SOURCE: Adapted from Philip Kotler, *Marketing for Nonprofit Organizations,* 2d ed. (Englewood Cliffs, N.J.: Prentice-Hall, 1982), 289.

the fruit of an apple—may be books, audio cassettes, videos, and so forth. Tangible products have up to five characteristics:

- *features* content designed for the beginner, intermediate, or advanced student
- *packaging* books, audiotapes, videotapes, and computer programs
- *styling* colorful, well-designed, and appealing package
- *quality level* physical condition and accuracy range anywhere from excellent to poor
- *brand name* reputation of the publisher or producer[2]

The augmented product is like the skin of the apple, holding it all together. Augmentation can include timeliness of access, accuracy of information, friendliness of staff, and so forth. For a product to be excellent, all three product aspects must be of high quality.

Product Assessment

In summary, it is crucial that products be assessed from a variety of perspectives and regularly evaluated during the annual planning cycle. In addition, library staff need to become comfortable with the concept of the product life cycle. The criteria outlined in figure 6-4 can be useful to the process of assessing both present products and ideas for potential products.

Once each present and potential product is evaluated, those products appearing to be the most appropriate to community needs—and, therefore, in support of the library's goals and objectives—must be assessed one more time in the light of the twin factors of cost and demand. Of course, this is not possible until the cost to produce each product is calculated, which is the focus of discussion in chapter 7.

It is important to recognize that regardless of budget allocation size, there is considerable flexibility available to the library. Product lines and product items can be either expanded or contracted, depending on marketing audit and cost/demand analysis results. Figure 6-2 illustrates how this flexibility can be practically implemented.

Figure 6-4   Assessing Products

Market Factors	Criteria
Information agency operations	Compatibility with agency efforts—really our business Continuity—would not require interruption of present activities Availability of general know-how Ability to meet customer service requirements
Potential market	Market size/volume Location Market share (present and potential) Diversity—needed by several target markets? Assured market growth Stability in lesser budget years Foothold in a new field, area
Marketability	Estimated cost vs. competition Presence of qualified personnel Ease of promotability Suitability of existing distribution channels Originality of product Degree of competition (present and potential) Life expectancy of demand Customer loyalty Absence of opposition from competition
Production	Feasibility of product Adequacy of technical capability Development cost Adequacy of production capability Materials availability Staff availability Equipment/space availability Service support availability Storage availability
Budget	Effective return on investment Capital availability Payback period

SOURCE: Adapted from Darlene E. Weingand, *Marketing/Planning Library and Information Services* (Littleton, Colo.: Libraries Unlimited, 1987), 67–8.

Although this discussion may seem reasonable in terms of present products, the development of future products may seem more obscure. In the next several pages, we will look at the futures strategy of scenario building to help in the design of potential library products.

The Mandate for Scenarios

Since the late 1960s, the practice of using scenarios to forecast possibilities has spread from military use to other governmental agencies and then to industry. The military used scenarios to propose war plans, such as: "How will our forces respond if this or that combination of enemy forces attacks in manner X or sequence Y?" The military then tested its plans by "playing out" responses through maneuvers and simulated war games.[3] This approach allowed planning for a full range of contingencies.

In contrast, most library planning has been done based on a single set of assumptions about the future. Because every future is filled with multiple possibilities or alternatives, selecting just one to plan for the future has proved to be both inaccurate and limiting. Incorporating scenario building into the planning process would enable library staff to explore more fully a spectrum of "what ifs" as the process proceeds.

In addition, the rapid pace of change has been causing fluctuations in a whole series of environmental areas that must be taken into consideration during planning. These fluctuations first become evident in the marketing audit but must also be monitored between audits if the library's external environment is to be accurately assessed.

> *Social* Shifting attitudes and grass-roots movements have significant impact.
>
> *Political* Laws and regulations, triggered by changes in political philosophies, continually alter the civic and institutional landscapes.
>
> *Economic* Inflation, deflation, increases and decreases in the cost-of-living, downsizing—all these "blips" on the fiscal screen have major ramifications.

Ecological   Rising concerns about the environment versus corporate interests create major confrontations.

Technological   Particularly in libraries, developments in technology fundamentally alter how business is conducted.

With significant changes occurring almost daily in all of these areas, it has become more difficult to plan effectively. Some of the errors in planning that have surfaced have been based on one or more of the following, and scenario building can make planning more realistic and comprehensive:[4]

Assumption of rationality   Individuals and institutions will act in accordance with traditional value systems, conventional wisdom, and "reasonable" behavior as understood by the planners. If library staff subscribe to the notion of the "goodness" of the library and the expectation that the library will receive support because the library is a public good, they may be in for considerable surprise. Today, demonstration of benefit and accountability are far more powerful arguments for funding than inherent worth. Scenarios reflecting rational, supportive, indifferent, and hostile funding situations can inform the planning effort.

Belief that the world is kindly inclined   Plans often assume optimistic environments and outcomes. This error, too, is rooted in the "goodness" philosophy. As economic constraints become more severe, simple worth will not achieve political success. Scenarios depicting expected "best-case" and "worst-case" possibilities need to be developed during the calm of the planning process when emotions are not engaged.

The implementation of incremental changes only   The library may neglect the consequences of drastic shifts and changes. If the library staff opt for the expected set of incremental changes and ignore the possibility of large-scale change in one or more areas, the completed plan may prove of little value. Building scenarios covering multiple degrees of change in a variety of arenas can prompt new product development and expand the range of the planning effort.

Omission of inputs other than economic   The library may ignore the effects of social reactions, political actions, environmental developments, or technical developments. Product design is affected by funding, to be sure, but many other environmental attributes also have powerful impacts to be considered. If the library's products are truly going to be responsive to community needs, all inputs need to be represented, and the scenario- building process is an effective way to do so.

Quantification only for economic data   This leads to failures to specify the degree of change, even if a social, political, etc., change is recognized. Since economic data are largely numerical, the temptation to quantify can be overwhelming. However, aspects other than economics are equally important and need to be considered in qualitative terms. Scenario construction is fundamentally qualitative and provides an excellent balance and counterpoint to sheer numbers. Therefore, library staff can gain considerable benefit from incorporating both approaches into the planning process.

Rejection of unpalatable events and trends   The library will lose potential opportunities (the flip side of threats). It is human nature to prefer positive over negative, but it can be both short-sighted and dangerous to turn a blind eye to possibilities that one simply does not wish to acknowledge. "Surely it isn't possible that our library is losing community support?" "It can't be that our budget will be cut by 25 percent—the library is so important to the community! (We think.)" But these unpleasant possibilities must be faced, and scenario building can be a helpful and nonthreatening way to do so.

Devaluing low-probability events to the point of discard   This can backfire when the unanticipated does, indeed, happen. Even low-probability events should be incorporated into the scenario construction process—"low probability" does not mean "*no* probability." For example, if the library staff believe that the local economy is basically sound and plan with that assumption in mind—and then a local major employer shuts down, putting hundreds of people out of work—there is nothing in the plan that can help with this sudden turn of the wheel of fortune. A series of scenarios depicting a range of economic possibilities would have prompted some contingency planning.

Neglecting societal reactions to situations   Here the library fails to explore how its important customer groups will respond to the complexities of conditions. If the customer is to be the focus of library service, then ignoring customer reactions would seem to be inexcusable. Scenario construction must reflect not only the library's response to changing conditions but also potential customer response that, in turn, should be mirrored by additional library response.

Because our world is now so highly interactive, a single plan can no longer suffice. Therefore, it is vital that a series of disparate possible futures be developed; scenarios fulfill this requirement.

Futures Strategy: Scenario Writing

While the word *scenario* may sound sophisticated or complex, it is really as simple as telling a story. It is simply a series of events that we imagine happening in one possible future . . . and then another future . . . and yet another. A scenario answers the basic question, "What would happen if *XXX* occurred?" For example, "What would happen if our library provided Internet access for the public?" Once the question is asked, creative minds can begin to imagine a range of sequential actions and consequences related to the event.

A more-formal definition for a scenario is "a description of events that might possibly occur in the future." A scenario is normally developed by

- studying the facts of a situation
- selecting a development that might occur
- imagining the range and sequence of developments that might follow

Frequently, families of scenarios are developed describing a given set of events. One scenario might be "best case," in which positive events occur; another might be "worst case," in which everything goes wrong; yet another might take the middle road. In each case, the scenario would attempt to depict what life would be like given the particular "future history" represented by those events that do occur and those events that do not. Then the consequences of various possible combinations of events are carefully studied.[5]

What can a scenario do for library planning? First, it makes us aware of potential problems that might occur if we were to offer the proposed product (or take the proposed action). We can then either abandon the action or prepare to take precautions that will eliminate or minimize the problems. Second, the scenario gives us an opportunity to escape from a negative situation or make it work to our advantage. For example, offering Internet access would incur an ongoing expense that we might not be able to afford . . . but partnering with an Internet access provider could not only reduce or eliminate this cost but would also offer another opportunity for interagency cooperation.

Third, the scenario can get others involved in assessing a situation and planning action. It is much easier for many people to focus on concrete situations in which the "what if" question begins the discussion. It is also important to recognize that a scenario is hypothetical, and "however good our futures research may be, we shall never be able to escape from the ultimate dilemma that all of our knowledge is about the past, and all our decisions are about the future."[6] Certainly, the future is always fundamentally unknowable—which is another very good reason for exploring alternative futures in the process of planning and sorting out the options.

To discover what the library's planning options might be, scenarios can be used to help define trends that are[7]

> *probable* but *"shapeable"* (at least regarding their impacts on the library), such as legislative trends
>
> *probable* but *not amenable* to library influence (such as demographic changes)
>
> *possible* and *"shapeable,"* such as developments in technology
>
> *possible* but *not amenable* to (or worth the effort of) library influence, such as weather and climate

This is proactive behavior at its finest: timely internal adaptation to developing external trends and planned external action to help shape those trends as much as possible.[8]

Developing Scenarios

Because scenarios are hypothetical sequences of events intended to focus attention on causal agents and potential outcomes, they need to be regarded as process tools rather than sources of data. Scenarios contribute in two primary areas:

> suggesting how precisely some hypothetical situation might come about in sequence
>
> identifying what alternatives exist, at each step, for preventing, diverting, or facilitating the process[9]

One of the main values of creating scenarios is to create a sensitivity to the possibility of alternative futures, leading to a willingness to experiment with strategies that will affect outcomes. Those developing the scenarios are forced to think in terms of events and interactions among those events—a way of thinking that might not otherwise take place. It is a time when creative problem solving is a necessary ally and adds much to scenario construction.

Harvey Welch Jr. and Sally E. Watson, in their discussion of techniques of futures research, propose three main approaches to the construction of a scenario:[10]

1. The first type is *based upon consensus and uses the Delphi Method to elicit expert forecasts for a specific time frame.* (See chapter 5.) The scenario grows out of this combination of expert opinions. This type of scenario does a good job of postulating events; however, those constructing the scenario have the challenge of developing the interactions and consequences of those events, relating them to the library and its environment.

2. The second method is that of *iteration-through-synopsis,* involving the development of different scenarios in multiple disciplines. The scenarios are combined and massaged until the resultant scenario comfortably accommodates the various elements. This method can be particularly

valuable for libraries, as many of the scenario elements will come from outside the immediate information field. A broad range of contributing elements can be very helpful in developing interrelationships between the library and its various constituencies.

3. The third method generates a scenario by using *a cross-impact technique,* testing the effect of one aspect of the scenario on all of its contributing parts. (For further discussion of cross-impact analysis, see chapter 7.) This method can be combined with the other methods and used as a way to construct the necessary interrelationships among scenario elements.

It does not matter which method of development is used as a baseline for discussion. The scenario writers need to build a wide range of alternative scenarios, focusing on the one (or few) that most directly depict desired and preferred futures. Where conflict between the present and the selected scenario(s) exists, a window of opportunity is defined, and library staff can take action to work toward making the preferred scenario unfold. Two caveats, however, need to be factored into scenario construction: The resultant scenarios must be fundamentally realistic and contain sufficient elements of plausibility and internal consistency to be believable, and personal bias must be guarded against.

The key to effective scenario writing is a willingness to have an open mind and consider possibilities that may seem unreasonable, impossible, or totally unrelated to libraries. An added bonus is that scenario writing is fun, and the discussions that produce scenarios can be stimulating and intellectually invigorating. Thinking about "what if" questions can illuminate both current issues and potential outcomes to be considered.

Product Ideas through Scenario Writing

Using scenarios to develop potential product ideas can be a stimulating and inventive exercise. Figure 6-5 illustrates "best-case" and "worst-case" examples in this scenario-building process. Methods of scenario building outlined previously can also be applied to this "best/worst case" model. An illustration of such an

Figure 6-5   Evaluation of a Product through Scenario Building

Proposed Product Idea	*"Best Case" Possibilities*	*"Worst Case" Possibilities (requires problem solving)*
Community Internet access	Partnership with local Internet service provider	No local Internet provider available
	Work with local library system	Library not a system member
	Library budget can support	Library budget cannot support
	Partnership with local schools	Schools do not wish to participate; have own system
Multitype library delivery	Develop a service funded by participating libraries	Local libraries cannot support with existing budgets
	Secure start-up funding through grants	Proposals not funded
	Service guarantees daily delivery	Present interlibrary loan service takes 5–14 days
	Service becomes entirely self-supporting	Library boards do not view the library as a business
24-hour reference/ information access	Partnership with library system libraries to spread responsibility	Not all system libraries willing to participate
	Electronic reference with guaranteed 8-hour response time	Library budget insufficient
	Librarian wears beeper	Staff unwilling to wear beepers
	Library staff rotates hours to provide 24-hour service	Union will not allow such staff rotation

application can be found in figure 6-6. Data elements for this model are initially generated using the Delphi Method. The Delphi Method results are massaged in several ways, as specified in the following list. Scenarios developed in this way proceed from a product idea into various implementation possibilities.

Figure 6-6 Applying Methods of Scenario Building

Proposed Product Idea	*Method 1: Using Delphi*	*Method 2: Multiple Disciplines*	*Method 3: Cross-Impact*
Community Internet access	Invite groups of experts to suggest strategies for providing Internet access Five such groups might be computer experts, librarians, telephone/communications experts, funders, citizens When the Delphi study is completed, rework the results into a scenario	Scenarios can be developed using the data generated by each of the groups identified in Method 1	Each identified scenario element is entered on a grid, and the effect(s) of each upon the other(s) is proposed and noted

- A single composite scenario is written. (method 1)
- Scenarios are developed within separate groups. (method 2)
- The data elements are arranged in a cross-impact matrix to discuss possible consequences of each element upon the other(s). (method 3)
- "Best-case" and "worst-case" scenarios are cast.

Another approach to using scenarios in product design is to start scenario development by asking a more general question, such as "What information needs will my community need in 2005?" Responses to this question, using the Delphi Method or other means of data collection, can be used to propose products that may or may not be in current use. Figure 6-7 demonstrates how this approach can be applied.

Using scenarios to generate product ideas or to propose possible implementation strategies allows the planning team to "try on" the new suit before buying—or assess whether a presently owned suit can be remodeled successfully to be fashionable. While this clothing metaphor may be stretching the concept a bit, it makes the relationship between scenario construction and product design more concrete.

Figure 6-7   Starting with a Broad Question

Question	*Identified Elements*	*Possible Products/ Distribution*
"What kind of information needs will my community have in 2005?"	Internet access	Library provides access Library joins local Freenet Library cooperates with vendor
	24-hour access to library	Shared cost with library system Computer access Library staff wear beepers
	Rapid receipt of information	24-hour delivery service Computer delivery to home

Assuming that the planning team now has worked through the scenario development process and assuming that product ideas have been generated, the marketing element of pricing/cost must be added to the mix. Chapter 7 addresses price/cost in terms of cost-benefit analysis and the two futures methods of trend extrapolation and cross-impact analysis.

THOUGHTS AND MUSINGS

What products does my library offer to our customers?

Are these products directly responding to identified customer needs? How?

Should new products be added? Which ones?

Should any products be phased out? Which ones?

Should any adjustments be made in the product mix, product lines, or product items? If so, what?

What are the areas of duplication with other agencies? What are the opportunities for cooperation?

Notes

1. Philip Kotler, *Marketing for Nonprofit Organizations,* 2d ed. (Englewood Cliffs, N.J.: Prentice-Hall, 1982), 289.
2. Philip Kotler and Alan R. Andreasen, *Strategic Marketing for Nonprofit Organizations,* 3d ed. (Englewood Cliffs, N.J.: Prentice-Hall, 1987), 423–7.
3. James R. Bright, *Practical Technology Forecasting* (Austin, Tex.: The Industrial Management Center, 1978), 256.
4. Bright, 257.
5. Howard F. Didsbury Jr., *Student Handbook for the Study of the Future* (Washington, D.C., 1979), 34, 177.
6. Ian H. Wilson, "Societal Change and the Planning Process" (paper presented at the annual meeting of the American Association for the Advancement of Science, New York, 31 Jan. 1975), 6, as quoted in Ian H. Wilson, "Scenarios," in *Handbook of Futures Research,* ed. Jib Fowles (Westport, Conn.: Greenwood, 1978), 226.
7. Ian H. Wilson, "Scenarios," in *Handbook of Futures Research,* ed. Jib Fowles (Westport, Conn.: Greenwood, 1978), 229.
8. Wilson, 229.
9. W. L. Brewis, "Futures Studies and the Future of the Library," *Mousaion: Journal for Library and Information Science* 10, no. 1 (1992), 34.
10. Harvey Welch Jr. and Sally E. Watson, "Techniques of Futures Research," in *Utilizing Futures Research: New Directions for Student Services,* ed. Frederick R. Brodzinski (San Francisco: Jossey-Bass, 1979), 9–10.

7

Cost-Benefit Analysis

Using Trend Extrapolation and Cross-Impact Analysis

To fully assess whether a product should continue or be developed, the cost (Kotler's *Price* as explained in chapter 1) to produce that product must be known; therefore, these cost factors must be identified. No business would offer a product for sale without knowing what the costs were (and, therefore, have the ability to judge what the price should be). Yet, libraries routinely operate without having this information. While libraries have had budgets, they typically have been of the line-item variety, and the costs for each product have not been calculated. This has made decision making regarding what products to develop, which ones to downsize, and which ones to eliminate virtually a subjective exercise.

Every business—and the library should be considered a business—works with both direct and indirect costs. Direct costs are those expenditures that can be attributed to specific products, while indirect costs are those expenses that relate to the library's total operations. While direct costs are relatively easy to identify, indirect costs are more difficult to assign to individual products because they support several (or all) products. To be able to

Figure 7-1   Examples of Types of Costs

Direct Costs	*Indirect Costs*
Rental of space or equipment	Operation of buildings and equipment: rent, heat, light, maintenance, and depreciation
Salaries of personnel hired to work specifically with a particular product	Salaries of permanent library personnel
Supplies purchased in support of that product	Supplies from existing stores normally kept in stock
Promotional expenses	Supplemental services, such as municipal or institutional purchasing, billing, and printing

compare products on a cost basis, both direct and indirect costs must be known. Figure 7-1 gives examples of both direct and indirect costs. Later in this chapter, we will discuss how these costs can be determined.

The Foundation: Program Budgeting

A direct relationship exists between cost factors and the budgeting process—and the structure of that process. There are many types of budget formats, and many funding authorities have specific requirements as to which format must be followed. However, it is the program budget that yields the most information for planning and decision making. The program budget identifies and arranges costs by specific program/product. Good reasons to create a program budget include the ability to

> evaluate present and potential products by comparing costs
>
> describe in detail exactly how the funds will be spent
>
> document which products might be phased down or eliminated if funding were reduced
>
> communicate to customers what products could be available to them if sufficient additional monies were provided[1]

In program budgeting, each product carries its own minibudget for direct and indirect costs. These individual budgets can be merged to create a condensed budget entry for another budget format. Even if the library's funding authority requires a line-item budget, it is a simple and straightforward procedure to take the sum of similar categories in a series of program budgets and insert that sum into the corresponding category in the line-item structure. For example, take all of the personnel entries from the spectrum of program budgets and add them together to produce a line-item total for personnel. There is a significant advantage to library management when the personnel costs for each product are known in addition to the overall personnel figure; the program budget provides this information.

Although it is admittedly more time-consuming to develop a program budget than to construct a basic line-item budget, the time spent is a good investment. In addition to providing necessary information for the marketing/planning process, it can be very beneficial to the library when both types of budgets are presented at the annual budget hearing, with the program budget serving as the basis for the presentation.

How Can Costs Be Assessed?

To identify the cost factors that become components of a program budget, cost-finding methodology of some type must be used. Each known product (for example, reference service, the collection, or circulation) must be broken down systematically so that each cost can be associated with an output. This is the opposite of planning a new program, where the desired output would be stated and the resources necessary for that output would be estimated to arrive at a budget. It is a useful exercise to examine a known product to learn to recognize those factors that must be considered when planning a new program.

When doing cost finding, the product/program being examined must be clearly defined, with a designated output that reflects the goal and objectives to which that product relates. This is the moment when the planning and marketing processes become deeply intertwined. Each objective in the library's plan requires the implementation of one or more products to achieve that objective. Once product definition has taken place, the costs can be identified and calculated. The final step is to ascertain the relationship between cost and benefit once all cost factors are known.

Therefore, for each product/program, both direct and indirect costs must be identified; some of these are fixed (known and stable) and some are flexible (adjustable or negotiable).[2] Direct costs can be apportioned to each product in a relatively straightforward manner since they represent cost elements that are directly incurred as each product is developed. However, indirect costs are more elusive and require more careful identification, and formulas, such as those found in *Cost Finding for Public Libraries,* can be useful in doing the calculations.[3]

For those who are "mathematically challenged" or not interested in working with numbers, there is a "shortcut" approach to allocating indirect costs using a process based on the distribution of staff time. Through the use of a time log, the time each regular staff member spends on each product is recorded and weighted according to staff salary. The sum of weighted time spent by the entire staff on each product can then be calculated as a percentage. Each product percentage can be individually multiplied against the expenditures in each of the library's indirect cost centers, with the results inserted into a program budget.[4]

The Demand Side of the Equation

There is another lens—besides cost—to look through when deciding which products to offer, even when information from the marketing audit and relative cost factors are known. This lens is *demand.* One of the outcomes of the marketing audit is an indication of anticipated demand for each present and potential product. This projected demand is then weighed against the identified cost factors. A proposed product may be very cost-effective and may help to respond to an identified need, yet the reality of demand may not be apparent. In this situation, it may be helpful to institute a trial period for a new product to determine whether appropriate demand will be forthcoming.

To reach effective decisions regarding which products to offer to the community, each product offered by the library must be assessed in terms of cost and demand. Figure 7-2 presents a working diagram in which both aspects are presented. The

Figure 7-2   The Relationship between Cost and Demand

High demand High cost	Low demand Low cost
Low demand High cost	High demand Low cost

shaded areas represent the need for serious problem solving, as a product in high demand that carries a high cost, or a product that only costs a small amount but is in low demand, cannot receive an automatic "green light" without serious consideration. The unshaded areas are another matter: a high-cost product with low demand can (and should) be readily discarded, and a low-cost product in high demand is every librarian's dream.

It is not an easy matter to decide which products are to be offered. With adequate information available, however, the library manager can make product decisions that will correlate with the planning process and that will be realistic in terms of cost and demand. Without the necessary data concerning cost, demand, and the relationship between the two, vital information would be lacking and subsequent decisions less well-conceived. True accountability is more than fiscal stewardship; it is grounded in informed decisions based on identified needs, cost factors, documented demand—and customer benefit. Figure 7-3 lists some pertinent product-analysis questions.

What Is Cost-Benefit Analysis?

Calculating costs in isolation without investigating the consequences or benefits that a present or proposed product might bring to the customer is of marginal usefulness. A product might

Figure 7-3   Product-Analysis Questions

Primary Question	Secondary Questions
What is the competition?	Is there duplication of this product by some other agency or group?
	If so, can my library do it better or for less cost?
	Is there potential for growth in the target market so that more than one provider of this product is reasonable?
	Should we provide this product?
What is the involvement of the target market?	How important is this product to the target market right now?
	Is there a preexisting relationship between the target market and the product?
How complex are the information-gathering and decision-making processes?	Are library resources available to undertake this analysis of market relationship to product (assuming that this analysis is beyond the capability of the marketing audit)?

SOURCE: Adapted from Darlene E. Weingand, *Marketing/Planning Library and Information Services* (Littleton, Colo.: Libraries Unlimited, 1987), 81–2.

be quite reasonable to produce and, regardless of the size of customer demand, be of only marginal effectiveness if customer convenience factors are not considered. Cost-benefit analysis examines the full range of cost factors necessary to produce a library product, including both direct and indirect costs—plus the intangible costs such as time and convenience. In addition, the analysis identifies present and potential benefits of that product to the library's customers. These two sides of the equation—cost and benefit—are determined for each of the library's existing and proposed products so that an overall analysis of product desirability can be made.

Kotler quotes Adam Smith in stating that, "The real price of everything, what everything really costs to the (customer) who wants to acquire it, is the toil and trouble of acquiring it." He expands upon that statement by suggesting that there are three costs to be added to actual production cost: effort costs, psychic costs, and waiting costs.[5] To put these concepts into a library context, consider the following costs of connecting the customer with the product:

> cost to the library to purchase the material
>
> staff cost required to acquire and process the material
>
> indirect costs associated with the operation of the library
>
> customer's time, cost, and trouble to physically go to the library (if required)
>
> or library's cost in getting the material to the customer
>
> customer's anxiety over when—or if—the material can be secured
>
> customer's wait until the material is available or arrives
>
> "intangibles" that accompany the transaction, such as speed, convenience, timeliness, accuracy, staff attitude, and so forth[6]

These more-subjective aspects of cost significantly affect the benefit (or lack thereof) part of cost-benefit analysis.

Kotler further contends that "consumers balance the expected benefits from an action against the expected costs." He states that "the nominal money price tag on the exchange may be the least important of the perceived costs the consumer is concerned about."[7] (Perceived costs in the library context may be found in figure 7-4.) Unfortunately, such perceived costs do not come readily to mind when library staff are considering product ideas. However, they *are* important cost components and must be deliberately inserted into the product-development process.

Cost-Benefit Analysis and the Ratio between Cost and Demand

When cost-benefit analysis is used in assessing product ideas, rather than just a simple costing model, the focus is appropriately on the customer. Demand for a product will rest not only upon the excellence of the product itself in its various aspects

Figure 7-4 Customer View of Cost Benefits

Perceived Costs	Examples
Time involved to make a request	Getting to the library
	Waiting in line or on the telephone
	Returning again if the item was unavailable during original visit
Potential embarrassment	Requested information/item deals with a sensitive topic
	Requested information/item does not support the self-image the customer wants projected (for example, checking out a trashy novel)
Aggravation	Enduring heavy traffic
	Busy reference or circulation librarians
Awkwardness	Having to ask for assistance

SOURCE: Darlene E. Weingand, "What Do Products/Services Cost? How Do We Know?" *Library Trends* 43, no. 3 (Winter 1995): 405.

but also on the benefits (or lack of benefits) perceived to be derived. If product benefits, either present or anticipated, are not readily apparent to the customer, there will be little or no demand generated. The same is true of products that might appear to the customer to be potentially beneficial—but are too inconvenient to access. High subjective costs can reduce demand that might otherwise be present.

Therefore, consideration of both monetary and subjective costs are essential to product analysis. Monetary costs will be of significant concern to the library; subjective costs will matter to customers. This simple reality helps to explain why an otherwise excellent product (from monetary cost and quality perspectives) might not generate an anticipated demand. Focusing on the customer and those subjective costs can save time and effort when working on product design.

The next portion of the chapter addresses how two different futures strategies can be used in the product-design process. The first, trend extrapolation, considers how the future can be discovered by extending the present.

Futures Strategy: Trend Extrapolation

Trend extrapolation is one of the most-popular methods for exploring the future and also one of the simplest. This method takes a single trend and extends it into the future. Robert Ayres, author of *Technological Forecasting and Long-Range Planning*, explains that the "underlying supposition is simply that the 'environment'—or the balance of forces—does not change, so that it is reasonable to assume that the behavior of the recent past is a good model for the behavior of the near-term future."[8] In other words, trend extrapolation assumes that environmental factors will remain constant and that past trends serve as the markers for the future.

The existing trend, which must be expressed numerically, is plotted graphically over time as a solid line. The future projection is depicted as a broken line. Figure 7-5 illustrates trend extrapolation as an indicator of future population to be served by the library. Upon close examination of this graph, a potentially "fatal flaw" becomes evident. The graph assumes (as stated above) that environmental conditions will remain unchanged. There is no provision made for the influence of other external forces, reversals in the trend, and so forth. In addition, no causation is indicated or even considered.

More-sophisticated extrapolation models can be used, such as the S curve.[9] Such a model enables the forecaster to extrapolate from smaller, contributory trends and does not assume a continuing, consistent environment. Individual curves are plotted to represent established trends, and a dotted S-shaped curve is used to represent future developments. Figure 7-6 uses this multiple-trend model to illustrate the potential effects of both new industry and plant closings on community population (in an admittedly very simple format). When the rate of change is variable and the trends are complicated, this more sophisticated trend extrapolation model can be helpful and has the advantage of acknowledging "limits, leveling-off periods, and periods of rapid growth."[10]

The strengths of trend extrapolation methods include low cost, ease of interpretation, simplicity of construction, and a high level of reliability.[11] Trend extrapolation is probably the least complex forecasting tool to understand as well as a natural adaptation of human cognitive processes. Data requirements

Figure 7-5   Trend Extrapolation Model for Community Population

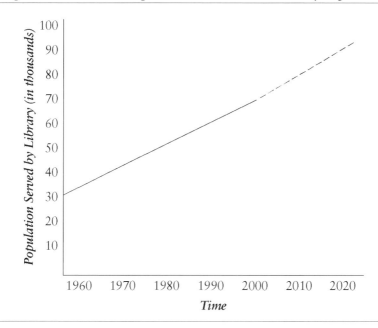

Figure 7-6   S-Trend Extrapolation Model
for Community Population

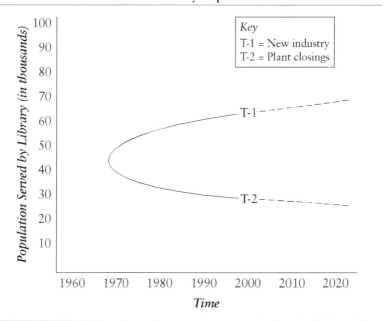

are minimal, and the standard historical, demographic, economic, or other statistical compilations can be used to acquire all the necessary data. The method definitely provides an improvement over using pure speculation and verbal argument about the future; however, as a systematic method, it requires more precision in identifying phenomena of interest so that one or more trends can be plotted. It also forces the researcher to learn more about past practice in order to forecast the future.

The simple exercise of closely examining historical trends can provide insight into the possible course of tomorrow's trends that might not otherwise be acquired.[12] Speculative questions that can support this exercise include the following:

- What will be the consequences if this trend continues unabated for X years?
- What will be the consequences if this trend levels off or accelerates from its current rate of increase?
- Which forces acting to maintain this trend are likely to remain constant, and which are likely to change in the future?
- If we wish to alter this trend in a particular direction, what determining variables might themselves be manipulated to do so?

Finally, when the focus turns to explanation of trends, the question of causal relationships must be confronted. Consideration must also be given to potential correlations to other phenomena—which leads us to discussion of cross-impact analysis.

Futures Strategy: Cross-Impact Analysis

Many forecasting techniques, including trend extrapolation, suffer from a basic limitation: They produce an isolated forecast without consideration of the possible influence of events and trends on each other. For example, a projected new library building carries a budget as part of its funding authorization. The expectation is that this budget is realistic and will support the requirements of the building plan. Simple trend extrapolation was probably used (even unconsciously) in the development of this budget. However, the "real world" of building construction and schedules may present a quite different set of conditions because interaction among events and trends is the norm rather than the exception. Therefore, some method for recognizing how separate events could cause impacts upon each other was necessary, and the strategy of cross-impact analysis was developed. Figure 7-7 illustrates how, in the example of the new library building, such a project can have an impact on—and be impacted by—other potential events, including new automated-system technology, repaving of streets around the library, and a budget cut of 10 percent.

**Figure 7-7   Linkage among Events Displayed
in a Cross-Impact Matrix**

If this event occurs	*The effect on these events would be*			
	Event A	Event B	Event C	Event D
A. New library building		+4	0	0
B. New automated system technology	+4		0	0
C. Repaving of streets around library	+2	+2		0
D. Budget cut of 10 percent	+2	+2	0	

The occurrence of a new library building (A) would greatly increase the likelihood of implementation of a new automated system (B) but would have no effect on the repaving of streets (C) or the budget cut (D).

The new automated system (B) would have a significant impact on the design of the new building (A) but no effect on the repaving (C). The budget cut would not be related because both the building and automated system would be funded from the capital budget.

The repaving of streets (C) would have an impact on construction of the library (A) and installation of the system (B) because access to the site could be compromised. There would be no effect on the budget cut (D).

The budget cut (D) would have an impact on the supplies, personnel, and other noncapital budget lines but not on the capital budget that funds the building (A) and automated system (B). However, a small effect is indicated to reflect the noncapital impact. There would be no effect on the repaving (C).

SOURCE: Adapted from John G. Stover and Theodore J. Gordon, "Cross-Impact Analysis," in *Handbook of Futures Research*, ed. Jib Fowles (Westport, Conn.: Greenwood, 1978), 303.

As a futures strategy, cross-impact analysis is both flexible and relatively easy to use. There are seven major steps in the use of cross-impact analysis as a method for projecting future situations.[13]

1. *Define the events to be included in the analysis (typically between 10 and 40 events).* It is important to include all pertinent events without succumbing to the temptation to include nonessential events. These events can be identified by searching the literature and interviewing key experts in the areas being considered.

2. *Estimate the initial probability of each event.* Probabilities should also include in what year the event is likely to occur. Each event probability is considered independently, without regard for potential influence by other events.

3. *Estimate the conditional (or impacted) probabilities for each event pair (two events considered in relationship to each other).* An estimate of strength and direction of impact is made. Statistical calculation of probability is normally done; seeking the expertise of a local mathematician or statistician may be very helpful here.

4. *Perform a calibration run of the cross-impact matrix.* Computer analysis can be used once the matrix of probabilities has been completed. A calibration run consists of randomly selecting an event for testing, comparing its probability with a random number to decide occurrence or nonoccurrence, and calculating the resultant impacts on all of the other events. Computer and statistical expertise are essential to perform this step.

5. *Define the policies, actions, or sensitivity tests to be run with the matrix.* In sensitivity testing, a probability estimate is selected about which uncertainty exists. In policy testing, an anticipated policy or action is identified that would affect the events in the matrix.

6. *Perform the cross-impact calculations for the policies, actions, or sensitivity tests.* For both policy and sensitivity testing, the judgments or policies are changed to reflect immediate effects. This can be done by either

changing the initial probabilities of one or more events or by adding a new event to the matrix. A new run of the matrix is then performed and compared with the initial calibration run. Any differences are the effect of the identified policy or judgment.

7. *Evaluate results.*

These steps may appear to be overly complex, particularly to the "statistically-challenged." This does not make the cross-impact technique any less useful as a forecasting tool. Even without statistical manipulation, considering each event in the light of other likely events and the possible impact each may have on the other is a powerful lens through which to examine products and cost-benefit. Whether rooted in statistical probability or common sense and intuition, the cross-impact approach is helpful for improving staff understanding of the potential interactions among the events being studied.

Merging the Strategies

The analysis of monetary and subjective costs can be greatly enhanced through the use of a cross-impact approach. As a present product is being evaluated or a new product is proposed, both financial and customer-convenience aspects need to be thought through. These aspects, along with proposed policies and decisions, can be entered into a cross-impact matrix, and probabilities can be adjusted until the most acceptable outcome appears. This is a more sophisticated tactic than is normally attempted in managerial circles, but the end result focuses on the most positive outcome—and demonstrating outcomes and impacts is very much in the forefront of today's accountability requirements.

In chapter 8, the discussion shifts to the connection of customers with products in an increasingly electronic environment. It is assumed that the products to be distributed have been rigorously evaluated and that attention on distribution is now the order of business.

THOUGHTS AND MUSINGS

Do I know what it costs to produce each product that my library offers to the community?

If yes, then do I consider both cost and demand factors when making product decisions?

If no, what steps can I take to identify these factors?

What budget format am I required to submit? If a program budget is not already my library's preferred format, what are the benefits and constraints to be considered if I wish to also track costs in this format?

Do I tell funders and the community what the library could provide if more funds were available? Do I routinely submit such a "blue sky" budget along with my required budget?

How can cost-benefit analysis be used to inform library decision making?

What trends can I identify in my community? How might these trends affect library operations in the next five years?

Do I consider the consequences of each action that is taken (cross-impact analysis)?

Notes

1. Darlene E. Weingand, *Managing Today's Public Library: Blueprint for Change* (Englewood, Colo.: Libraries Unlimited, 1994), 138.

2. Weingand, "What Do Products/Services Cost? How Do We Know?" *Library Trends* 43, no. 3 (winter 1995): 403.

3. Philip Rosenberg, *Cost Finding for Public Libraries: A Manager's Handbook* (Chicago: American Library Association, 1985).

4. Darlene E. Weingand, *Marketing/Planning Library and Information Services* (Littleton, Colo.: Libraries Unlimited, 1987), 67–8.

5. Philip Kotler, *Marketing for Nonprofit Organizations*, 2d ed. (Englewood Cliffs, N.J.: Prentice-Hall, 1982), 305.

6. Weingand, "What Do Products/Services Cost?" 404.

7. Philip Kotler, *Strategic Marketing for Nonprofit Organizations*, 2d ed. (Englewood Cliffs, N.J.: Prentice-Hall, 1982), 450–1.

8. Robert Ayres, *Technological Forecasting and Long-Range Planning* (New York: McGraw-Hill, 1969), 35.

9. P. Dickson, *The Future File: A Guide for People with One Foot in the 21st Century* (New York: Rawson Associates, 1977), 74.

10. Dickson, 74.

11. Dickson, 74.

12. Kim Quaile Hill, "Trend Extrapolation," in *Handbook of Futures Research*, ed. Jib Fowles (Westport, Conn.: Greenwood, 1978), 269.

13. John G. Stover and Theodore J. Gordon, "Cross-Impact Analysis," in *Handbook of Futures Research*, ed. Jib Fowles (Westport, Conn.: Greenwood, 1978), 305–13.

8

❦

Distribution in an Electronic World
Using Decision Trees

As explained in chapter 1, the third component of Philip Kotler's "*P*s" to directly influence product decision making is *Place*: how each product will connect with the target markets, the customers. Kotler refers to Place as how the library distributes its products—a definition that seems logical and reasonable when the customer secures the product at a single location.[1] The concept of Place becomes more complex when there are multiple access points, including both physical sites and other alternative delivery systems. Therefore, it is necessary to examine Place in the context of product distribution through channels of connection between products and customers. Obvious costs are connected to distribution and access, and decisions regarding cost-effectiveness and customer convenience will need to be made about which channel(s) within a range of alternatives will be selected for each product.

How Do Libraries Distribute Products?

The library has historically been viewed as a building or other physical space: a place to which library users would come to locate and check out materials or to read and study on-site. The quiet stacks provided a feeling of comfort and security for the user and a sense of order and harmony for the librarian. This mystique of hushed learning, which focused on books and other printed materials, was appealing to the regular user but often became a barrier to a casual seeker of information—particularly to anyone whose learning style was not print-centered or who struggled with a learning disability.

The concept of library as a place is rooted in the institutional aspects of library operations and continually re-creates the image of the library as a building, a physical structure that houses and preserves the records of knowledge. Consider an important question: Is the library a building containing resources of sufficient value that present and potential customers will both use it and support its operation? Too often, libraries are used on a regular basis by only a minority of the population served. This level of usage is often reflected in economic support, and the level of funding for libraries is frequently under challenge. Fiscal constraints and budget cuts are more the rule than the exception.

While this is a discussion of place with a lowercase *p,* it is related to the Place spoken of by Kotler, and both words refer to physical location and its extensions. Today, the concept of Kotler's Place incorporates both tangible space and whatever distribution channels are established to connect the customer with the product(s) desired. The previous image of library as building has a decreasing validity in today's increasingly electronic world, and those who seek to perpetuate it as the image of choice are doing a disservice to the library's effectiveness in serving customers. The library that seeks to foster an image of being essential to the community and on the cutting edge of information provision cannot afford to be tied exclusively to yesterday's paradigm of service.

Figure 8-1   **Examples of Products and Potential
Distribution Channels**

Product Example	*Possible Distribution Channels*
Best sellers	Library building
Interlibrary loan	U.S. mail delivered to home or office Pick up at library building
Material reserve request	Telephone Computer generated
Obtaining reserve material	Pick up at main library building Delivered to home or office
Information request	Telephone Computer access In person
Story hour	Library building Cable TV program

There are many options for distribution in the library's tool-box; some of these are presented in figure 8-1. As illustrated, the same product could be accessed through more than one delivery mechanism. Selection of the appropriate channel(s) should be driven by what has been learned in the marketing audit about customer convenience needs. Figure 8-2 illustrates how customers' information needs can be met through a variety of distribution options. Traditional channels may work perfectly well under certain circumstances; other situations may require electronic or other types of connections. The keys to designing appropriate delivery systems are the consideration of flexibility and customer convenience every time a product is offered to the library's community.

Therefore, we must remember that the library can be viewed either in its "institutional" role as the storehouse of a product with intrinsic value or as a point of intersection between human need and relevant data.[2] If the desired outcome of library service is the satisfaction of customer needs, it seems reasonable to propose that distribution channels should be designed to respond to the various attributes of customer satisfaction.

Figure 8-2 Connecting Customers and Library Products

Customer	Information Need	Distribution Options
Hospital worker who works 11 pm–6 am shift	Wants to locate hotels or motels in the Southwest before leaving on vacation	Worker goes to library during open hours to get materials Worker locates materials via computer access and has them delivered to local branch Librarian faxes information to hospital
Stock broker who works 10 am–6 pm	Wants to learn French before attending a conference in Paris	Broker goes to library during open evening hours (Tues. and Thurs.) Broker locates materials via computer access and has them held at desk Library refers broker to "French for Travelers" course at high school
Single parent of pre-schoolers with full-time job and children in day care	Looking for materials on parenting	Parent takes children to evening story hour and while waiting, looks for parenting materials Librarian suggests attending a young singles parent group that meets in the library
Retired teacher with mobility problems	Looking for tours to Europe that make special provisions for people with disabilities	Volunteer delivers library materials Librarian contacts tour companies specializing in special access tours and refers customer
Third grader who is dyslexic	Has school assignment on dinosaurs	Librarian finds information in audio and video formats; child picks up at library Librarian locates Web sites; child does research from home
Industrial worker who works 3 pm–midnight shift	Hopes to buy a camper; wants consumer information	Librarian provides information via telephone Worker goes to library and examines consumer magazines Librarian refers customer to local camper dealers

Determining Channels of Distribution

Without framing distribution within the concepts of customer convenience and access, subsequent decision making might be unduly influenced by cost considerations or by bowing to tradition. However, when convenience and access are proposed as the desired outcomes, objectives and actions can be written that will move the library toward developing distribution channels that meet customer needs.

To make realistic distribution decisions, nine decision factors should be considered. With convenience and access as parameters of the library decision frame, these nine factors must be included in the ongoing discussion and evaluation process. In addition, these factors are also presented as a response to the essential question: How does electronic access and transmission change traditional distribution?[3]

FACTOR 1

Quality of Service

Distribution must be viewed as an integral component of each product, for a product that cannot be used by the customer is of very little value. Therefore, when the qualities of customer convenience and access are at a high level, the product itself is enhanced. This interdependence of product and distribution can be observed in several use measures: the nature of the information output (level of accuracy, language, appropriateness, etc.), the format in which the product is available (audio, print, visual, person-to-person, program, etc.), the type of access (building, electronic, mail, etc.), and the speed of obtaining the desired information. (See chapter 6 for discussion of core, tangible, and augmented products.)

FACTOR 2

Time, Convenience, and Resource Allocation

The increasing onslaught of sensory images and daily demands that besiege each of us produces an environment in which time and convenience needs feel so real that we could almost touch them. It is not surprising then that perceptions held by the library's customers regarding product excellence will be strongly influenced by the personal time that they must expend to secure needed information. This time element can be defined as the

> *time expended by staff in the process of providing information* A well-educated and trained staff working with appropriate library resource materials and knowledgeable in the skills of referral can retrieve the needed information efficiently and with minimum expenditure of time. A staff that has experienced less training or has fewer resources available may require more time to search out what is needed—and may ultimately be less successful.

> *time expended in overcoming physical distance between customer and service* The most efficient staff and the most comprehensive collection of materials cannot be of service to the customer until a connection can be made between the customer and the desired product. The traditional notion of the library solely as physical space becomes less and less the norm in the light of the increase in daily demands facing customers and a corresponding decrease in their personal time. To address these constraints, it is imperative that multiple access points be established. These multiple points can include such options as satellite physical sites, electronic networks, telephone service, and mail/delivery services; tomorrow's technologies will provide still more options.

> *real time that service is available to the customer* The prior two dimensions of time can be dealt with through careful management of tangible resources. However, *real time* must be defined as clock hours—the number of hours and location of those hours within the twenty-four-hour day—that the library's products are available to customers. Consider several questions:

> - How many hours per day?
> - Which hours?
> - How do the present or recommended hours correlate with the hours available to customers?

- Are there ways to effectively use technology to overcome time limitations?

Careful analysis of these questions, as informed by the data gained from the marketing audit, can provide a real-time access profile that could be both efficient and effective.

FACTOR 3
Priorities and Planning

When an overall framework of marketing is used to guide the planning process and the setting of priorities, the spotlight focuses on the customer. However, even under these auspicious circumstances, it is important that customers become "stakeholders" in the entire process by inviting representatives from the various target market groups to be members of the planning team so that they can participate at every stage of the process. In this way, there is continual input from customers, and access considerations can be updated as customer needs change.

FACTOR 4
Human Resource Intermediaries

Access can also be addressed through cooperative arrangements and ventures between the library and other agencies or organizations. Examples of possible areas for cooperation might include

- cable television operations linking information agencies and individual homes or offices
- computer networks
- shopping malls (establishing a satellite physical outlet)
- postal/mail services for delivering materials
- experts in needed areas such as finance, law, fundraising, technology, etc.
- human service agencies
- government agencies

These collaborations can expand the effectiveness of participating agencies and diminish areas of duplication. In terms of accountability and political influence, cooperation is definitely to be valued in today's information age.

FACTOR 5

Number and Location of Outlets

The word *outlet* is used here as a descriptor for buildings, bookmobiles, storefront locations, kiosks, or even a small room with a computer workstation. The emphasis is on a facility that serves as an access point between the customer and needed information. Customer convenience needs, as determined by the marketing audit, must be the guiding factor. Both existing and potential service outlets should be assessed at regular intervals in conjunction with planning-process deliberations.

FACTOR 6

Technological Delivery and Formats

The principles presented in discussion of Factor 5 also apply to outlets that are accessed through technological application. The rate of technological development is accelerating so rapidly that new possibilities for distribution are continually entering the marketplace. Today's world includes cable television, interactive video, computer networks, teleconferencing, broadcasting systems, satellite transmission, facsimile transmission, videotext, and many combinations and permutations of these technologies.

However, the mere existence of a technology does not ensure that it is appropriate for implementation in a particular library; yet, it deserves serious consideration and evaluation as one of a number of delivery options. It is interesting to note that in a time of rapid societal and technological change the same developments that cause change may hold the key to coping with change.

New information formats in such arenas as audio, video, and optical technologies offer expanding possibilities for customers with special learning styles and needs. Different formats, both individually and in combination, are also basic to the storage and retrieval of information. Both storage capability and speed of retrieval are significantly enhanced by technological development, and libraries will be forever influenced and altered by present and emerging technologies.

Innovation and Change

All of the previous factors coexist in an environment of change and a corresponding need for innovative responses to change. If access to information is to remain in step with the needs of a world that must survive in the present and prepare for the future, the willingness to experiment with alternative ways of thinking, coping, and responding is a mandate for library survival. The library manager who wants to be part of the information mainstream must learn to be proactive in the distribution of information and to be personally receptive to change. Innovation is generally considered to be a small tail on a normal bell-shaped curve; moving closer to this innovator extreme is a challenge to be embraced in the dawning of a new century.

The Finite Life Cycle

The concept of a finite life cycle applies not only to products but to all aspects of the marketing mix including cost, distribution, and promotion. All components of the mix have applications that are "born" in response to customer needs; they have a peak period of effectiveness, experience a decline, and ultimately must give way to more-appropriate applications. This natural ebb and flow inevitably picks up speed as change accelerates.

Positioning

There are two levels of positioning: identifying the market niche for the library within the broad range of information providers and developing distributed products that also have a unique market share among the many possible competitors for customer attention. The underlying assumption is that the library and its products cannot and must not be expected to meet all possible human needs. Discovering the best market placement for the library is a responsibility and a challenge that no library manager can afford to ignore.

These nine factors are central to distribution decision making and should be carefully thought through as part of the effort to develop creative and flexible approaches to information service. Placing the library's products in the marketplace is a complex endeavor, and customer needs must govern distribution design and implementation. In addition, adding creativity and risk-taking to the process can place the library in a strong, proactive position to effectively move forward into the future.

Futures Strategy: Decision Trees for Distribution Decisions

Of the full range of futures methods that could be applied to library decision making, the decision tree works well for considering potential channels of distribution. Related methods include relevance trees and contingency trees. All three "trees" attempt to illustrate graphically the logical relationships among actions and events. The major difference is that decision trees and contingency trees tend to highlight branch points where choices and alternative decisions can be made. Relevance trees focus on the importance of input to the general outcome.[4]

The tree approach is most useful as a visual categorization of choices and alternatives. It is similar to the process of flow charting in that it presents information in graphical terms. While this presentation can clarify choices for everyone involved, it can be particularly useful for those decision makers whose preferred learning style tends toward the visual.

Futuristics, or futures studies, can be particularly helpful in assisting the decision-making process. Some benefits, with examples relating to the tree approach, include[5]

Providing useful frameworks for decision making and planning Everyone operates within a set of assumptions. If these assumptions are erroneous, planning can become a disaster and decisions may be entirely off track. For example, if a library staff sits down to create a planning document without first engaging in a marketing audit, a scenario could be drawn and extensive goals and objectives put into play to serve a target market that is disappearing. Using futures methods can help provide reasonable assumptions about what the future may be like, even though those assumptions must be viewed as possibilities or probabilities. In addition, it may become apparent that certain assumptions need to be periodically reviewed as time moves forward.

Identifying future dangers and opportunities Both threats and areas of potential development must be recognized so that appropriate action can be taken. If these are not identified—at critical junctures for achieving success—accomplishments that might have been will not occur. For example, if the library is planning a new system upgrade and does not discover that a significant new enhancement will be available in six months, the opportunity to negotiate for this enhancement may pass.

Suggesting a variety of possible approaches to solving a problem In addition to the framework for decision making discussed in the preceding two paragraphs, the tree method is particularly useful for looking at a spectrum of approaches. See figure 8-3 for an example of using a decision tree to explore distribution options for a story hour. In this example, there are four major "branches" on the tree: audience, possible channels, possible venues, and staffing. The following discussion explains how figure 8-3 can be interpreted:

- *Audience* Story hours can be developed for any age of audience. To what age group is this story hour to be directed? Possibilities include preschool, K–3, junior high, high school, and adult.

- *Possible channels* There are a variety of ways to connect the story hour with its audience. How will the story hour be delivered? Possibilities include the traditional in-person, face-to-face experience; a program prepared for cable TV; a video that is prerecorded and subsequently circulated from the library's collection; and a prerecorded audio cassette that also is made part of the collection.

- *Possible venues* Story hours can take place at different locations. Where will this story hour take place? Possibilities include in the main library's children's area; in a branch library; at a cooperating agency, such as a nursing home or day care center; and at the cable TV studio.

- *Staffing* No program takes place without staff, and levels of staff must be considered. What staff will be used? Possibilities include the children's librarian, a professional storyteller, library support staff, and volunteers.

Figure 8-3   Example of a Decision Tree

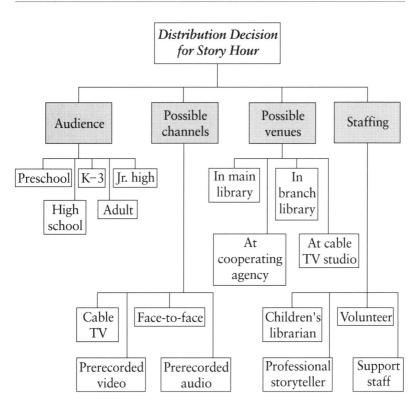

Helping to assess alternative policies and actions   In addition to identifying possible approaches, the decision tree method promotes discussion of possible future impacts. Too often, distribution decisions are made without thought of consequences, which can be hazardous in the long term. Using the tree methodology to identify alternatives and forecast impacts can result in better distribution decisions. If a library seeks to expand its small-business market and identifies a range of potential distribution channels for connecting customers and information, it could well stretch its resources beyond reasonable limits. Using a decision tree can target many options—including increasing levels of service and charging for extended service—that may meet small business needs and safeguard library resources.

Enabling people to see the present   People normally base their decisions on what they believe the present to be. However, perceptions of present conditions are frequently biased toward the past, and the past colors the present. This can be particularly problematic regarding distribution decisions, as the lure of tradition is a powerful one. Perceptual lags, such as occur in the library struggling desperately to maintain a full range of children's programming in spite of the fact that the population of young children has diminished markedly, can be costly. The decision tree might identify technological applications that could suggest a viable strategy for continuing a program while expending fewer library resources—or suggest other programmatic endeavors.

Increasing the degree of choice   When people don't recognize that they have alternatives, they tend to be fatalistic about what is possible. Too often, library staff will express thoughts such as, "We tried that once, and it did not work." By using a decision tree to identify other possible developments, staff gain a sense of freedom of choice and do not feel locked into the present situation. In addition, because people are fearful of change, exploring a range of choices can make the journey into change seem less threatening.

Today's world requires that creativity and risk-taking be brought to the distribution decision-making process. Yesterday's methods of distribution are still considered possible choices, but a much broader range of options are available to the library—and more are on the way. Decision trees can help library staff harness their creativity through identifying alternatives and considering subsequent impacts. In this way, decisions can be made that have the greatest potential for success in tomorrow's world.

Successes need to be communicated to the library's community. In chapter 9 avenues of promotion are considered.

THOUGHTS AND MUSINGS

How are my library's customers connected to the products produced by the library? How effective are these connections?

What mechanisms are in place to find out from customers if our present distribution channels are reaching them?

Are all the decision factors considered when we are making distribution decisions?

If no, what steps can I take to incorporate more of these factors into our planning process?

If yes, have we identified areas where improvement is needed?

How can I use decision trees to help in making distribution decisions?

Notes

1. Philip Kotler, *Marketing for Nonprofit Organizations* (Englewood Cliffs, N.J.: Prentice-Hall, 1982), 321.

2. Brenda Dervin, "Useful Theory for Librarianship: Communication, Not Information," *Drexel Library Quarterly* 13, no. 3 (July 1977): 16–32.

3. Darlene E. Weingand, *Marketing/Planning Library and Information Services* (Littleton, Colo.: Libraries Unlimited, 1987), 98–107.

4. Harvey Welch Jr. and Sally E. Watson, "Techniques of Futures Research," in *Utilizing Futures Research*, ed. Frederick R. Brodzinski (San Francisco: Jossey-Bass, 1979), 12.

5. Edward Cornish, *The Study of the Future* (Washington, D.C.: World Future Society, 1977), 220–1.

9

Promotion

Using Emerging Avenues of Communication

Promotion is one of the final steps in the marketing/planning process. However, decades of confusing rhetoric have clouded the meaning—and opportunities—that this set of activities offers to the library manager. This confusion lies at the heart of the definition of *marketing* in the minds of librarians. Although the word *marketing* frequently appears in library literature, it is presented in language that really refers to *Promotion*, Kotler's fourth P (as explained in chapter 1). However, this is much like the "tail wagging the dog" because promotion is not set in motion until all other marketing and planning components (except final evaluation) have been completed.

In this chapter, *Promotion* is defined as "communication"— the library communicating to its customers that community needs have been identified and that cost-effective products and methods of distribution have been developed to respond to those needs. The tone of these messages is informational rather than the sales approach so popular in the typical marketing literature.

What should be promoted? Two additional questions can shed light on the answer to that question:

What library product or service has relevance to your customers' needs as determined by a marketing audit?

What outcome is desired?[1]

When considering the response to these questions, remember that while all promotion is communication, not all communication is promotion. Promotion can be viewed as "communication with an attitude."[2]

To further explain: a product should be actively promoted when the

> product is efficient, reliable, and responsive to identified customer need
>
> desired outcome is either an increase in usage, a redirection of usage, or a deeper understanding of the service in general[3]

The reverse situation—transmitting routine communication rather than active promotion—occurs in those instances when the

> library is unable to provide the level of service required to meet an identified need
>
> library cannot absorb or handle a major increase in workflow in a particular service area
>
> product or service is administrative, such as a policy change[4]

Therefore, considerable communication takes place both in routine daily activities and in a promotional effort. However, in either mode it is important to recognize that the attributes of the communication process affect what the library has to say, how it transmits that information, and how the messages are received.

The Communication Process

Communication may seem relatively straightforward, but it is a more-complex endeavor than many people believe. To fully understand how communication takes place, it is useful to consider the basic communication model. There are eight basic components in this model (see figure 9-1).

The *sender* initiates the message and selects the form of transmission. The jagged lines represent the interference or dissonance that the sender may be experiencing due to other environmental factors, such as worry, interpersonal strife, or fatigue.

Encoding translates the thought into some type of symbolic form (such as words, pictures, sounds, etc.).

The *message* carries the content of what is being transmitted.

Channels are the paths through which the message moves between sender and receiver. These paths can include speech or various media formats (such as print, audio, video, etc.).

The *receiver* is exposed to the message from the sender. Jagged lines are again presented here, as dissonance may also be affecting the receiver.

Decoding by the receiver translates the message into interpreted meaning.

The *response* from the receiver incorporates the interpretation that the receiver created after being exposed to the message.

Figure 9-1   The Communication Model

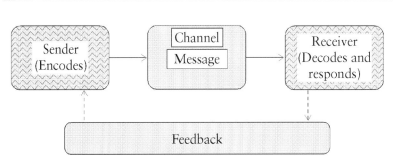

Feedback is that part of the receiver's response that is communicated back to the sender. The feedback loop is not automatic and must be deliberately designed into the overall process.

Regardless of the identity of the sender or receiver or the type of channel selected, basic communication transpires in the same sequence illustrated in the diagram. The two places in the sequence where the model can break down are the degree of dissonance experienced by the sender or receiver and whether a feedback loop has been built into the process design. Both of these conditions can disrupt the communication process, and care must be taken to minimize any disruption.

Thoughts about the Audience

If the basic communication model is to be used effectively in promoting the library's products, the target market(s) or audience for each message needs to be clearly identified so that appropriate content, style, and media are selected. In figure 9-2, suggested communication channels or locations for distribution are presented in relation to specific target markets. For example, if the aim is to reach teenagers, putting promotional spots on the local easy-listening stations will probably not be effective, but use of stations that play the music enjoyed by this age group should be successful.

As another example, many libraries produce newsletters that they then distribute via mail or some other means to their communities. In this day of desktop publishing, why don't libraries publish several versions of the newsletter, each version targeted to a specific market group? Some articles will be unique; others can be slotted into several newsletter versions. With segmented mailing lists, no additional mailing costs would be incurred. This example merges traditional and contemporary promotional approaches and promises a more-positive outcome.

A segmented approach can also be applied to the library's annual report. Too many libraries forfeit an excellent promotional opportunity when they either do not prepare an annual report or prepare only what legal or funding authorities require (which usually consists of entirely numerical data). The annual report

Figure 9-2   **Target Markets and Potential Channels**

Target Market	*Communication Channel*
Teens	Rock radio station, MTV
Senior citizens	Easy-listening stations, classical stations, senior group newsletters, senior centers
Small business owners	Small Business Development Center, Chamber of Commerce, Rotary, Kiwanis
College faculty	Internet, faculty union (if applicable), campus library
College students	Internet, student groups, campus library

can be a very effective way of telling the library's story. The use of humor, photographs, graphics, and human-interest narratives can make the document entertaining and appealing. Creating different versions targeted to specific market groups can make the report more relevant.

In addition to adopting promotional strategies targeted to specific markets, it is also essential that a feedback loop be built into the process so that the audience's response to the message can be determined. In face-to-face conversation, feedback can be immediate, but in mediated situations, designing feedback is a more-complex undertaking. Strategies such as polls, return postcards, and surveys are possibilities for gaining feedback data.

Traditional Library Promotion

For decades, librarians have operated under a set of assumptions that no longer can be deemed entirely valid. Within these assumptions, the library was viewed as a public good and essential to the community's quality of life. Such assumptions can still be supported; the problem lies with subsequent assumptions that proposed that libraries "should" be supported because of their "goodness" and that people "should" use the library for their own "good." In today's world, this is where the argument falters. Today, the library's present and potential customers have increasing numbers of choices and more competitors for their time and support. Simple "goodness" will no longer suffice as a rationale for use; demonstrating customer benefit presents the only workable position from which to operate.

Using these outmoded assumptions as a foundation for management also led to a set of promotional behaviors that simply do not work in today's environment. Library staff routinely bought into the "build a better mousetrap" school of promotion: Provide good products and the community will "beat a path" to the library door. In support of this mind set, staff sent out press releases, wrote newspaper columns, put up posters and displays—all designed to "tell" the world what the library was doing. Figure 9-3 gives examples of some of these traditional methods and suggests newer channels of communication to consider.

The notion of asking customers what they need and want was rarely considered; after all, librarians were the professionals, weren't they? And who "should" know better what the public "should" want (to read)? In other words, the conceptual struc-

Figure 9-3　Examples of Promotional Channels

Product	Present Channel(s)	Potential Channel(s)
Reference service	Bookmarks	Selective dissemination of information (SDI) Word-of-mouth Media spots
Interlibrary loan	Librarian suggestion	Bookmarks Media spots Web page
Story hours	Newspaper column Posters	Local teachers Media spots Parent-teacher organizations Day care organizations Balloons
Computer-access (OPAC)	Signs in library	Telephone message Media spots Bookmarks

ture for promotion was very clearly defined, but this structure spoke to yesterday's assumptions and probably was not as effective—even then—as it could have been.

Facets of Promotion

The assumptions that need to be adopted to succeed in today's marketplace are very different from those of traditional library promotion. Rooted in customer service and perceived benefit, today's assumptions must focus on the customer's needs and convenience without any "shoulds" in place. The spotlight falls on the customer, not on the library. With these new assumptions as an operational mandate, the library can embrace a wide spectrum of promotional possibilities. The exercise of promotional strategies can be linked to a variety of potential facets.

To fully comprehend the multiple facets of promotion, a metaphor of promotion as a precious gem can be helpful. (See figure 9-4.) This metaphor allows us to view promotion as having multiple sides that need to be considered when selecting strategies for each individual product. One facet, or several facets in com-

Figure 9-4   The Facets of Promotion

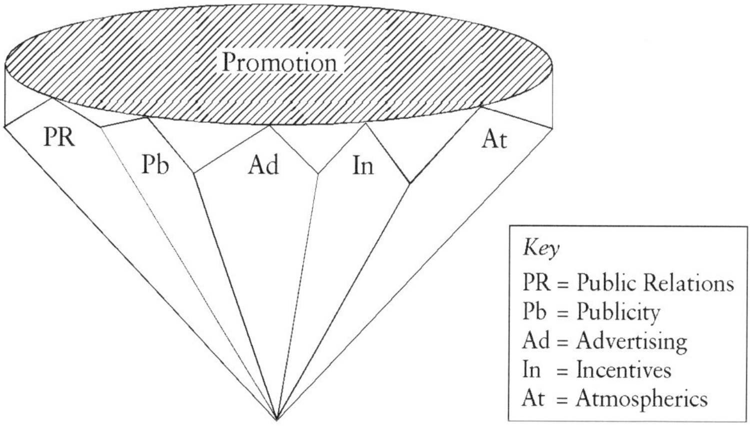

Key
PR = Public Relations
Pb = Publicity
Ad = Advertising
In = Incentives
At = Atmospherics

bination, may be incorporated in a promotional effort. As with the other components of the marketing mix, the focus of any promotional effort must be on the target customer group(s) if the message is to reach those for whom it is intended. Promotional facets include[5]

Public Relations   This facet covers the overall relationship between the library and its current and potential customers. Public relations reflects the mutual perceptions and attitudes held by both library staff and library customers. How the library is regarded in its community is a clear reflection of the public relations that are in place. Interpersonal contact is a primary ingredient of public relations because even an excellent series of product ideas cannot be implemented without human action and interaction. The quality of this interpersonal contact influences in large part how well the customer's needs and the product(s) offered correspond. The relationship between the library and its public is a cumulative one, with trust and mutual respect building over time. Like a garden, this relationship must be carefully cultivated and nourished; in both good times and bad, it is the library's greatest asset.

Publicity   News coverage of the library's affairs secured at little or no cost is considered publicity. Included in the repertoire of possible publicity efforts are press releases, newsletters, columns in local newspapers, media interviews, bookmarks, posters, displays, and Web sites. Publicity transmits information concerning the benefits of using the present or proposed library products. The range of possibilities is limited only by creativity and imagination.

Advertising   When publicity is paid for, it is generally regarded as advertising. Promotion in this form usually must be very sophisticated and contemporary to compete with other advertisements. However, it is possible to combine publicity and advertising by inserting a "bug"—a small, relevant note about some library activity placed within the body of a larger ad paid for by someone else! An example of a bug would be the insertion of a small promotional piece describing holiday food and decorating materials available at the public library that is placed within a full-page ad for the local grocery store. While advertising has not traditionally been a frequent type of promotion for libraries, there certainly could be times when it would be the most appropriate facet of promotion. It is also possible that local media may wish to contribute newspaper space or broadcast time as a public service.

Incentives Another facet of the promotional "gem" can be effectively used in the product market testing phase, when customer attention needs to be drawn to a potential product. Known as incentives, such strategies encourage customers to actively engage in the use of the product. Examples might be an improved interlibrary loan service via fax with coupons distributed for free faxes, an extended loan period for videocassettes, a free demonstration, and so forth.

Atmospherics Critical to promotional efforts and integral to good public relations, atmospherics include such elements as the ambience and environment of the distribution channels, whether physical sites or electronic connections.

- Are library buildings comfortable, with adequate heat and light?
- Is there adequate signage so that customers can move about confidently?
- Do customers feel welcome?
- Is there adequate staffing to serve customers?
- In the electronic world, can customers reach the library by telephone or computer without needing to redial?
- Is a menu of options available to lead customers to the service they are seeking?
- How reliable is the electronic connection?
- Is twenty-four-hour service available?
- Are customer needs met with fast and efficient results?

Atmospherics affect both attitude and perception and are essential to good customer–product interaction.

Customers "vote with their feet" and will choose avenues for gathering information that address their convenience and comfort needs, in addition to providing effective results.

These multiple facets of promotion enable the library staff to think creatively and view the entire effort as one in which options and choices exist. As new technologies emerge, the range of options grows wider and the decision making more complex.

Promotion Using the New Avenues of Communication

Rather than pairing promotion with a specific futures method, the approach taken in this chapter is to highlight the increasing numbers and kinds of possibilities that developing technologies offer to libraries. The twentieth century has seen many advances in technology, including fiber optics, communication satellites, and CD-ROM. Until recently, technological changes were mutually supportive in producing common forms of output: ink-on-paper, hard-copy journal, or all-electronic program. However, the latest round of changes now promises a new multimedia format, sharing characteristics of both print and electronic media. Rather than communicating to mass audiences, these new media have the potential to de-massify, and perhaps personalize, information consumption.[6]

Such a scenario presents a very different way of looking at how information is accessed, packaged, and distributed. It also suggests that promotional activities must also be redesigned to operate effectively in this new environment. If the library's customers are exploring new means of communication, then the library must move boldly forward and use the same technologies if communication is to be maintained. Admittedly, the world is changing so rapidly that it is very difficult—if not impossible—to be completely up-to-date, but this presents an even stronger argument for monitoring trends and trying to grasp the tail of the whirlwind!

A word of caution: This does not suggest that traditional means of promotion and channels of communication should be totally abandoned. As figure 9-3 suggests, both traditional and newer promotional strategies have a place in the total promotion effort. The key is to use the most-appropriate and potentially effective strategies after carefully analyzing the customer markets and determining how each customer group communicates and gathers information.

What's Next?

Edward Cornish, editor of *The Futurist,* states that, "One of the best reasons for watching trends and thinking about where they may lead is this: If we don't know where we are going, we don't know where we are." He explains that most people view the present world as "known," and the future as "unknown." He further argues that our ideas of what the world is like today are based on our past experience—making these ideas always somewhat out of date.[7] Cornish calls this condition "present shock," in which "the real present bursts into our mental conception of the present."[8] An example in the library's environment might be a local survey result that indicates that a high percentage of citizens own personal computers and would like to receive their information in that mode. The library may have been operating under the assumption that customers preferred to come into the library to access information and learn about what the library offers. These two sets of beliefs are on a collision course: the irresistible force (technological change) meeting the immovable object (library tradition).

Paying attention to trends not only provides insight into how tomorrow will be, it can also wake us up to an existing condition of which we were not yet aware. In other words, an observable trend may not be "about to happen"; it may have already begun, and no one has noticed. One example of such a trend is "convergence." Many newspaper columns and journal articles have made reference to the "coming convergence" between computers and communications. What has been mentioned less frequently is that this trend is well under way: The Internet can be accessed via the home television set; many appliances have computer chips in their operating systems; TV pictures can be transmitted via telephone lines. These are just a few examples. New developments will use convergence technologies to make "smart" appliances, clothes, and so forth—with the ability to help with problem solving.

An exciting future is just ahead, but the beginnings may well be already in our past. It is the responsibility of the library manager to pay attention to the legacies of the past and the roots of the future that lie there, to a present that reflects the past and opens a window to what tomorrow may bring, and to a future as yet undecided but with attributes that are worth working for.

Making It All Work

There are organizational attributes that will either help or hinder promotional efforts. Of primary importance are administrative supports consisting of organizational commitment and the monetary resources that provide adequate funding and staff for promotional purposes. Both types of support must be present because having either commitment or resources in isolation can result in an effort that lacks balance.

It is also beneficial if the responsibility for the design and implementation of promotional strategies rests with a single individual, even though a number of staff (paid and unpaid) may be involved with implementing the strategies. This centralization of coordination sends the message that promotion is a key library activity and not an occasional event. It also helps make the process a systematic one that can produce positive public relations for the library.

Throughout this book, the continuing discussion of the marketing process has highlighted the "4 *Ps*" of the marketing mix: Product, Price, Place, and Promotion, while pairing them with various futures methods or approaches. Marketing strategies are integral to overall good management; however, they cannot be successful without the monitoring and final analysis elements that are part of the evaluation stage. In the next chapter, evaluation approaches are addressed in the context of simulation gaming.

THOUGHTS AND MUSINGS

What promotional strategies is my library presently using?

Have we used our marketing audit to identify target markets? Do we tailor promotional messages for each market?

How well are these promotional strategies reaching their designated target markets?

Is feedback a normal part of our communication effort?

What communication channels are we presently using? Will they reach the desired audience(s)?

Are there new avenues of communication that should be considered?

Notes

1. Kelly Krieg-Sigman, "Kissing in the Dark: Promoting and Communicating in a Public Library Setting," *Library Trends: Marketing of Library and Information Services* 43, no. 3 (winter 1995): 419.

2. Krieg-Sigman, 419.

3. Krieg-Sigman, 420.

4. Krieg-Sigman, 420.

5. Darlene E. Weingand, *Managing Today's Public Library: Blueprint for Change* (Englewood, Colo.: Libraries Unlimited, 1994), 145–6.

6. Jim Willis, "The Age of Multimedia and Turbonews," in *Exploring Your Future: Living, Learning, and Working in the Information Age,* ed. Edward Cornish (Bethesda, Md.: World Future Society, 1996), 120.

7. Edward Cornish, "Using the Future to See the Present," *The Futurist* 31, no. 4 (July–Aug. 1997): 4.

8. Cornish, 4.

10

❧ ⚜ ❧

Evaluation
Using Simulation Gaming

This is an era of accountability in which shrinking funding and expanding needs require that libraries demonstrate their effectiveness to their communities and their patrons. Evidence must be routinely gathered and presented in quantitative as well as qualitative terms to make comparisons possible. These comparisons can be structured in two ways:

- between your library and other libraries of comparable size and activity
- between your library's present and past performance

There is nothing mystical about evaluating library operations. Too often the word *evaluation* conjures up images of numbers, statistics, and mathematics. A better approach might be to ask questions, such as: "Is the attempt to reach young adults working?" or "How good is this service?" The use of questions enables planners to think in more human terms about real problems and situations.

Developing this approach further, figure 10-1 illustrates the "Tell It!" framework, a model for developing an evaluation process. This model begins with the library's vision for the future and identifies a range of possible alternatives for achieving that vision. It also focuses on monitoring and communicating the progress that is made. Finally, what is learned is merged with the library's full product mix, and an assessment of needed improvements moves the library closer to the selected vision.[1]

Why Evaluate?

The question, "Should we evaluate the library and its services?" is not the issue; rather, the question is "To what end and to what

Figure 10-1   The "Tell It!" Framework

Talk about the vision	The difference we want to make is . . . For these reasons . . .
Explore alternatives and design your approach	The best way to do this would be . . . For these reasons . . .
Learn from what's happening	The way we'll check on progress is . . . We can correct for problems by . . .
Let people know what happened	The way we'll document the difference we've made is . . . We'll communicate the difference by . . .
Integrate results with ongoing services	We'll take what we learned and relate it to the library as a whole by . . . The best way to integrate learnings would be . . .
Think about how it all worked!	Improvements to be made in performance . . . Improvements to be made in planning

SOURCE: Douglas Zweizig and others. *The Tell It! Manual: The Complete Program for Evaluating Library Performance* (Chicago: American Library Assoc., 1996), 106.

degree should we evaluate?" In this complex and changing world there is little time for action without a carefully reasoned rationale. In addition, accountability demands evaluative data to document the status and quality of library service. Adequate levels of funding and support require it, as "goodness" no longer garners necessary resources. Library survival depends on evaluation. Becoming essential to your community cannot happen without it.

Looking at evaluation from a slightly different angle, it is important to recognize that staff resources need to be conserved and nourished. Therefore, the available energies should be directed toward strategies having a reasonable expectation of positive results. Routine evaluation can provide both the informing data and the framework for charting where staff efforts are best spent. This is an often overlooked benefit of evaluation, but one that can have significant impact on staff satisfaction and morale.

However, the results of evaluation may or may not please the library staff, and the possibility of demonstrated inefficiency and ineffectiveness certainly exists. This possibility only makes evaluation more important because detected inadequacies can be quickly corrected. Furthermore, if the data indicate that potentially unpopular actions need to be taken—such as extended or weekend hours, change of lunch hours, and so forth—the very existence of that evaluation data substantiates and supports the change mandate. A key to community trust and good public relations is that it is essential that suggested changes do take place when customers have been asked to assess services. If not, a public rationale should be given for the delay or inaction to maintain credibility with the community.

Types of Evaluation

Introduced as Postlude in chapter 1, two types of evaluation are normally used in assessing library products and services. The first type provides a monitoring function throughout the marketing/planning effort and is known as either *formative* or *process evaluation*. Process evaluation monitors progress toward achieving goals and objectives. Figure 10-2 suggests questions that can be used in the process evaluation effort. Figure 10-3 compares process evaluation to driving to New York City.

Figure 10-2   Comparison of Questions to Consider during Two Types of Evaluation

Formative/Process/Monitoring Evaluation Questions	*Summative/Summary/Final Evaluation Questions*
Are current measurement techniques adequately monitoring the rate of progress toward the objective? Should additional data be collected? How should this be done?	Is it a success or a failure?
Is movement toward achieving the objective on target? Is it behind or ahead of schedule? Are the expectations of progress still realistic?	Are the results positive or negative?
Should additional or different strategies be developed?	Will we want to do it again?
Should pilot projects be expanded to the entire library? Should experimental strategies be continued, expanded, or discontinued?	Was it worthwhile?
Are costs running close to original estimates? Are they adversely affecting any other library objectives or products?	Should we do it again?
Is the overachievement in any area adversely affecting other library objectives or products, or encumbering a disproportionate amount of the library's resources?	Can we do it again?
Is the objective becoming unrealistic or proving undesirable in terms of the overall picture of library services? Should it be modified or eliminated?	If we do it again, when should we do it?
Should new objectives be developed to better achieve particular library goals? Is the objective still relevant to the library's defined role in terms of itself and its community? Have any environmental factors changed? Is the development of new objectives or goals indicated to meet changing needs? Should the priority ranking among goals and objectives be revised?	What modifications should be made?

SOURCE: Adapted from Vernon E. Palmour, Marcia C. Bellassai, and Nancy V. DeWath, *A Planning Process for Public Libraries* (Chicago: American Library Assoc., 1980), 81, and from Darlene E. Weingand, *Marketing/Planning Libraries and Information Services* (Littleton, Colo.: Libraries Unlimited, 1987), 130–1.

Figure 10-3   Driving to New York City Evaluation Elements

Formative/Process/Monitoring Evaluation Elements	Summative/Summary/Final Evaluation Elements
Check map to decide what route to take	Was an appropriate route selected? Was it the most efficient route?
Check map to determine when to turn onto interstate	Should the interstate have been used? Could we have found out about the road construction in advance? What could we do differently next time?
Study map to assess progress	Should we have turned off the interstate and used local roads, given the amount of construction encountered?
Check map to see at what exit to turn off interstate	The exit we selected was closed due to construction; could we have foreseen this and exited earlier? (We had to go many miles out of our way.)
Check map to decide what local roads to take	We had to take different local roads than originally selected because our first exit was closed. This required additional checking of the map.
Monitor progress along local roads into New York City	Traveling on local roads was difficult due to rush hour. Next time, we should plan so that we avoid this busy time.

The second type looks back at the entire effort at the end of a fiscal year or a given project. Known as *summative* or *summary evaluation*, this is the final assessment that rates aspects of success or failure and informs decisions concerning potential replication of parts or all of the activities. This final evaluation judges whether the goals and objectives were achieved and, if so, whether the timeline for completion was on target. Figures 10-2 and 10-3 also suggest basic summary-evaluation questions and their relationship to process-evaluation considerations.

When the staff reflects on the program or service being evaluated, several factors can be considered as part of this discussion:

- techniques that were found to be particularly effective
- learning that occurred as a new service program was developed
- details that should be remembered when carrying out such a program
- hints for keeping a project on schedule
- ways of monitoring the budget to maintain control of expenses
- methods found useful for assessing the effectiveness of services[2]

Finally, the discussion can focus on improvements to be made, in performance and in planning. These improvements can help the library to breathe life into the mission and vision while creating an environment in which change is a welcome partner rather than a dreaded visitor. The next planning cycle can build upon these improvements, and successive cycles that evolve from strategic evaluation efforts will keep the library proactive and ready to move confidently into the future.

Futures Strategy: Using Simulation Games to Monitor and Assess Progress

Games can be constructed in many formats, including (but not limited to) the following: board games (Monopoly and Trivial Pursuit), computer games (Myst and Where in the World Is Carmen Sandiego?), in-basket games (see figure 10-4), and mental or pantomime games (Charades). Another category of games, simulation games, is used to create a hypothetical environment in which ideas can be tested. Gaming allows experimentation without the risk of "real" results, which can be an advantage. "Trying out" a course of action to gain insight into possible consequences can be very useful for informing decision making. Using simulation games can also add creativity and energy to the process.

Figure 10-4, presented at the end of this chapter, illustrates a simulation game that can help a library staff explore how the results of a community survey (targeting the library's hours of operation) can be evaluated and implemented under different conditions. Elements of cross-impact analysis are also incorporated into the process of the game through "sudden impact" events that occur and make adjusting library hours more challenging.

Simulation games serve four basic purposes, and it is not uncommon for several of these to be present in any given game situation. They serve to

- extract information
- transmit information
- establish multilogues among players (or planners)
- motivate players (planners) and prepare them for some future experience[3]

In the library context, all these purposes can be helpful in bridging the gap between evaluation results and needed improvements in operations. That is,

extracting information from evaluation results is essential to preparing it for use

transmitting information about the evaluation results provides needed input when considering modifications in operations

getting staff members to talk to each other about the results is key to developing a sense of ownership of both the evaluation process and the subsequent alterations to operations

having a sense of ownership is motivation in and of itself and generates enthusiasm for improving service

The choice of gaming as a strategy makes sense because games are a human phenomenon stemming from ancient times; game pieces have been found in graves dating back to the prehistoric era. While it is easy to assume that games should be classified as leisure activity, this is not the case at all. Games are universally found in all areas of human society, and they help meet human needs for recreation, competition, mental exercise, and education.[4]

Most people understand the recreational function best; games are fun. While they can admittedly be a means of escape from real-world problems, they also offer a risk-free environment for experimentation. In this context, games can be used as a highly motivating tool for learning—and for creating situations in which evaluation results can be hypothetically tested. This simulation attribute of gaming is not unlike scenario building; the difference is that certain established rules, boundaries, or procedures are in place.

The artificial framework of rules and activities governs the second function of gaming: competition. The degree of competition can be slight, as in "icebreaker" get-acquainted games; it can also be intense, as expressed in war games. For the library's purposes, the element of competition can be useful in comparing one potential improvement with another.

A third function of gaming is mental exercise, and a fourth function lies in education. Most games pose artificial problems requiring players to compete with each other or against the rules of the game. By simulating aspects of the real world (or by inventing fantasy worlds), gaming provides a unique opportunity for problem solving and, as a natural outcome, learning. Since problem solving is central to the marketing/planning process, using games to help bridge the gap between evaluation results and improvement decisions can be helpful indeed.

Designing a Simulation Game

Just as no one is born knowing how to write a questionnaire that effectively gathers desired types of data, no one automatically can design a simulation game. However, as discussed in the following sections, certain attributes need to be considered in the design effort—and additional insights can be gained through trial and error.[5]

Working Backward

Good simulation designers, like mystery writers, begin with a reasonable "solution" and work backward through a series of possibilities. In the marketing/planning context, the "solution" would be a desired goal or outcome. Feedback also must be part of the design so that the model feels real and players can draw linkages between their actions and real-world situations.

Target Audience

The designer needs to know the identity of the target audience for whom the game is intended. In the marketing/planning effort, this audience is the planning team. To create an effective design it is important to carefully assess the backgrounds and level of knowledge of team members.

Game Structure and Dynamics

Every game has a framework upon which the component parts reside; this is the *structure*. The game activities themselves are called *dynamics*. While many different dynamic and structural elements can be built into a simulation game, the most important are movement, time, scale, information, interaction, chance, decision, meaning, "chrome," components, rules, and conditions for winning. Most successful games contain many, if not all, of these elements.

Movement

There are two aspects of movement: the number of pieces a player can move in a single turn and the locations to which these pieces can be moved. A game board itself generally serves as a background upon which activity occurs. Sometimes the players themselves move from one location to another.

Time

Commonly used in simulation games as a framework for action, time affords the structure of discrete periods during which players undertake activities and make decisions. One variation that is suited to the use of gaming in marketing/planning evaluation is the "in-basket" exercise. Originally developed for business, this variation consists of tasks or problems "dropped" on the desk according to a set schedule. The players must not only solve the problems but also do so within the time constraints imposed by the game. Another aspect of time is the duration of the game, and the most effective simulations are usually those that can be played in less than eight hours and in one to two sessions.

Scale

Time and scale of game elements must be linked realistically so that activities required by the simulation can be accomplished in the time frame that has been established.

Information

Although all games involve an element of problem solving, simulation games have a much greater requirement for gathering information. It is common for simulation games to yield information only when certain activities are undertaken by the players and when there is much information to be potentially accessed. In other words, all the information players need to solve the problem is available—but only if the right questions are asked.

Interaction

For the purposes of working with the evaluation data, the most important element is interaction. Of course, interaction with the game itself is essential to gain needed information. However, extensive interaction among the players is the true core of the game. Such interactions may include planning, sharing, negotiating, buying, selling, and so forth. Even negative interactions, such as spying, treachery, and robbery, can be incorporated. Commodities such as goods and services can be exchanged. Intangibles such as information, trust, and goodwill are also important to include.

One way to achieve interaction that is particularly effective is the use of teams. The amount of interaction is thereby increased for individual players, while a single game experience is also achieved. A positive by-product of designing games for team play is the involvement of shy or disinterested staff. A shy staff member is not playing alone, and the enthusiasm of others can motivate those who claim no interest. In practical terms, teams of three to five are recommended—large enough to discuss an issue yet small enough to involve everyone, and an uneven number helps to resolve disagreements.

Chance and Decision

The chance function in gaming is to cause unpredictability. This is important in simulation games because reality is also unpredictable. The level of chance in a simulation game must be carefully calculated and the consequences of chance events evaluated. Any chance results that destroy either the simulation or a team must be avoided. A more-effective chance factor is the penalty that can limit a player's abilities or options.

Decisions are taken throughout the game that have consequences—a primary purpose of the game itself. Too much chance could make players believe that there is no link between decision and result, which would defeat the intent of the game as a learning tool.

Meaning

Every simulation game has a pattern: players trade, and one person/team gets more than all the others and wins. Good game design, however, adds enough real-world meaning so that the game is both interesting and educational. As an example, the library offers a range of products to the community in exchange for funding and support. To obtain this exchange, distribution and promotional strategies must be designed that are based on an analysis of community needs. Political factors also come into play, and teams must learn how the political factors operate, outguess built-in random elements, and help define the library's future. Such "real" concepts are learned within the parameters of the game through experimentation and planning based on the accessed information.

"Chrome"

Chrome is a peculiar word, to be sure, but one that describes those game attributes that augment meaning. For example, if game cards are used relating to local laws and regulations, these cards should be written in appropriate legal language to add to the realism of the game. Another example concerns levels of meaning. If the library in the game is seeking a budget increase and two city council members are closet ultraconservatives who personally object to some of the items in the library's collection, having that information could affect the direction that players may choose to take in presenting the budget. In other words, chrome is those details and twists of play that make a game more like real life.

Components

Components are the "nuts and bolts" of the game, ranging from a few sheets of paper to an elaborate game board. The driving principle should be simplicity, with the use of locally obtainable materials. However, components do need to look attractive and professionally produced as much as possible. Certainly, the availability of computers and desktop publishing makes game development easier than ever before. However, components that require labor-intensive behavior (such as the taking of notes, rather than the use of a preprinted form) should be avoided. Finally, since space is always an issue, the packaging of components must also be considered.

Rules

There is a balance between brevity and clarity that must be maintained. The rules should be easy to understand, with little jargon. Further, rules—like questionnaires—must be tested: The game should be played at least six times to "get the bugs out." Suggestions for improvement should be carefully considered and incorporated wherever they make the simulation better, more realistic, and so forth.

Winning

In designing the game for library staff, winning is not the issue. Rather, the simulation outcome sought is one of process: Which potential strategies would be most successful in bridging that gap between evaluation results and identified customer needs? The lack of clearly defined winning conditions makes it difficult to determine when the game has ended. If the end point has been clearly stated, players may try to improve their positions in the short term—a temptation to those who enjoy competition. Therefore, designing an end point that is unknown to the players can be a useful device that adds suspense to the game, keeps players focusing on the long term, and ultimately keeps the simulation from running on and on.

Tips for Encouraging Player Involvement in the Process

1. The moderator of a simulation game has sole authority to define the rules and resolve unexpected situations. However, the role should focus on encouraging player involvement and creativity.

2. The moderator must know the rules thoroughly, understand where the simulation is intended to go and what it is intended to teach, and personally play several rounds to "get the feel" of the game.

3. The players must adhere to the rules, but anything that does not seriously damage the simulation can be permitted. (However, if the players decide to solve the library's financial problems by winning the lottery, this probably should not be allowed because it would not encourage realistic problem solving.)

4. A high level of interaction may produce teams that encourage a competitive spirit. Even if promises are disregarded or truth is distorted as the teams compete, a "hands-off" approach is advised if serious damage to the simulation is not occurring. However, if emotions get out of hand, the moderator needs to defuse the situation and remind participants that it is "only a game."

5. The actual environment for playing the game should be comfortable, be without distractions, and include adequate supplies so that play need not be interrupted. The same location should be used when the game takes place in more than one session.

6. Continued participation is essential. The gaming process can collapse if key players do not return to the second session. This is also a good argument for using teams because substitutions can be made to teams without serious negative effect.

7. Fatigue can be a major concern. If a game is allowed to extend beyond four hours at one sitting, even the most interested and involved players can become tired. Overlong sessions should be avoided.

8. "Go with the flow" is a good slogan. Noise and activity are characteristics of player involvement. Repeated requests for assistance, particularly in the game's early stages, should be taken in order—even if a "take a number" process is needed.

9. Rules should be both read by every player and explained by the moderator before play begins. Playing a few practice rounds can help to place everyone "on the same page."

10. The moderator can inject "surprise" and "random" announcements of emerging conditions that affect the game—such as a $5 million bequest to the library or a bridge washout. Giving a five-minute warning that an announcement will occur gives players time to finish up immediate maneuvering.

11. The moderator should circulate among the players to ask about problems or the need for assistance. Hints can be dispensed if players are "stuck" or go off in a completely wrong direction. The moderator is a catalyst for successful play.

12. When the game has ended, a discussion session should be held, chaired by the moderator. Team members sit together. Participants or teams should be encouraged to discuss their results, their experiences during the game, their best and worst strategies, and what they learned. *This final step is possibly the most important, as it helps players internalize the experience and incorporate it into the marketing/planning process.*

Simulation Gaming in Marketing/Planning

One definition of simulation is "teaching through representations of real-life experience, not merely talking about experience, but actual participation while in the protected environment of the classroom."[6] The purpose of using simulation games in library situations is less the transmission of factual information—admittedly a legitimate function, as introduced previously—and more the development of "insights into the administrative and social processes surrounding library administration."[7]

Through another lens, simulation may also be defined as the "manipulation of a model to reproduce its operations on a set of data as it moves through time."[8] When the simulation adds the factor of time, an additional sense of realism is imparted to the exercise. This input of time can be particularly useful when cause-and-effect are the issues under discussion.

Combining the gaming environment with scenario construction is yet another approach in which a safe environment for testing ideas can be created. However, it is important to remember that while simulation has never been intended to be predictive, it can be an effective way to explore options and experiment with cause and effect.[9] Curiously, both evolving simulation theory and the emergence of planning as a managerial function in libraries have followed parallel developmental tracks.[10] When such a juxtaposition occurs, mutual reinforcement is a definite possibility. In addition, because appropriate planning and the use of simulation models are team activities, there is a natural affinity that can be exploited.

Another factor to be considered is experience, which is one of the most important tools required for real-world problem solving. However, gaining this experience can result in some negative outcomes and rigid views regarding change. While library situations cannot usually be considered in the "dangerous" category, there are still risks inherent in trying anything new.

In addition, since marketing and planning are managerial activities, they include extensive decision making. Because there are many parameters and contingencies that must be considered in such a decision-making process, the use of experiential simulation can create an artificial work situation parallel to the real world. The freedom thus gained in this secure environment allows decision making to break free from its traditional linear progression, bringing into play a wide range of ideas. Doing this experimentation within a simulation environment removes the real-world risks and fosters an opportunity for trying out multiple possibilities. The ability to envision a range of options is an invaluable managerial asset. A more-holistic and three-dimensional outcome can be the result.

Some of the reasons for developing simulation models include the search for an understanding of existing systems and the desire to forecast the probable reactions of a system to change. Such a systems approach encourages a view of reality as a series of interlocking parts—not unlike a puzzle—that are dependent not only on observable structure but also on interactions among the parts.[11] When working to develop marketing and planning strategies, the identification of potential puzzle pieces—and the range of scenarios that could be constructed—can expand the planning team's thinking and depth of response.

As an introduction to using simulation games in library staff development, figure 10-4 provides an outline of a potential game designed to work with the data gathered in an evaluation of the library's hours of operation. Teams of three to five staff members are formed. The charge to the teams is to prepare a five-minute presentation to be delivered at a special meeting of the library board that will make recommendations regarding changes in policies, procedures, and operations based on the evaluation results. To make the experience "real," special "sudden impact" events are read by the game moderator at ten-minute intervals in the first stage of play. Teams must adjust their deliberations to reflect the impact of these events.

Similar games can be designed in connection with evaluation of other types of library operations, such as products offered, customer service, delivery, and so forth. Again, the major advantage to using gaming is the creation of a safe and risk-free environment in which to experiment with possibilities and outcomes. In addition, gaming can effectively incorporate elements of cross-impact analysis, scenario-building, decision-trees, and visioning in its design.

Creating a simulation game to explore options for improvement of library operations is a complex, challenging, and creative activity. Success is directly related to knowing where one is headed—the outcomes desired. Although only a few minutes may be necessary to develop a rough draft of the game, it may take months to completely flesh it out. Looking at commercial simulation games with the intent of borrowing or adapting mechanisms that offer promise will provide a host of ideas. Ultimately, it is local data from the marketing audit that will provide the details necessary to produce a finished game. But in summary . . . this is a game, not a test. Players should be having fun.

Figure 10-4   Outline of a Sample Simulation Game Evaluating Library Hours of Operation

Game Element	Instructions	How My Library Can Adapt This Game
General description	An "in-basket" simulation, in which players receive information on a timed-release basis and then must make decisions in response to what they have learned	
Equipment required	An introductory letter from the director introducing players to the game and outlining the charge Evaluation results for the library's hours of operation "Sudden Impact" events, such as budget cut, fire in the library, crash of the online catalog, large bequest, etc. (approximately 10 events)	
Setup	Prepare the equipment components for distribution Divide staff by lot into teams of 3 to 5 players Seat teams with enough space so that team members feel comfortable discussing issues and keeping strategies confidential	
Initial briefing	Inform teams that they are about to undertake a simulation to design strategies building upon the evaluation results Give each team a copy of the director's letter and the evaluation results Direct each team to prepare a presentation to be given to the library board at the end of the first stage of play; tell the board what changes should be made in policies, procedures, and operations in response to evaluation results	
Stage 1 play	Moderator reads first "Sudden Impact" event; copies given to teams Every 10 minutes (or so), read another event, giving copies to teams In response to questions, advise teams that they can ask for whatever they want in their presentations Terminate Stage 1 after 90 minutes	

Game Element	Instructions	How My Library Can Adapt This Game
Rest break	10 to 15 minutes	
Stage 2 play	Inform all participants, except for the team making the presentation, that they are members of the library board (the game moderator is chair)	
	Encourage "board members" to adopt a "persona," such as politician, farmer concerned with tax increases, fire chief's spouse concerned with library getting more funds than fire dept., etc.	
	Encourage board members to ask questions, take notes	
	Randomly select a team to make the first presentation	
	Give each team 5 minutes for the presentation; at the end of 4 minutes, interrupt with "1-minute warning"	
	At expiration of that minute, ask board members if they have questions	
	No team answer may exceed 1 minute	
	When all teams have made presentations, declare Stage 2 ended	
Debriefing	Thank players for their efforts	
	Ask what they believe to be the strongest and weakest points of the presentations	
	Ask how they felt when speaking and answering questions	
	Ask if there were any difficult questions not asked or other issues that should have been covered	
	Encourage interaction among staff during this phase	
	Ask for discussion about what they thought the simulation was designed to do and what they got out of it	
	Ask for suggestions for improving the game	

The next, and final, chapter considers what has been learned about marketing and applies those ideas to thriving in the next millennium.

THOUGHTS AND MUSINGS

Is evaluation a systematic and regular activity in my library?

Do we evaluate not only at the end of a project or fiscal year but also monitor the process along the way?

If yes, how has the evaluation been useful in informing decisions?

If no, how can we institute such a routinized process?

Do we collect appropriate types of statistics so that we can compare ourselves with other similar libraries? With ourselves in prior years?

Staff frequently dislike collecting data. How can I persuasively demonstrate the benefits to the library that such data collection provides? What are the benefits to staff individually?

What steps could we take to design one or more simulation games to help us link evaluation results to the design of improvements in library operations?

Notes

1. Douglas Zweizig and others, *The Tell It! Manual: The Complete Program for Evaluating Library Performance* (Chicago: American Library Assoc., 1996).
2. Zweizig and others, 36–7.
3. Richard D. Duke, "Simulation Gaming," in *Handbook of Futures Research*, ed. Jib Fowles (Westport, Conn.: Greenwood, 1978), 355.

4. Peter Hamon, Darlene E. Weingand, and Al Zimmerman, *Budgeting and the Political Process in Libraries: Simulation Games* (Englewood, Colo.: Libraries Unlimited, 1992), 3.

5. Hamon, Weingand, and Zimmerman, 16–25.

6. M. J. K. Zachert, "The Design of Special Library Teaching Tools," *Special Libraries* 64, no. 9 (Sept. 1973): 362.

7. Zachert, 362.

8. Pauline A. Oswitch, "Computer Simulation for Library Management: A Rationale," *Encyclopedia of Library and Information Science* 41, supplement 6 (1986): 22.

9. Hamon, Weingand, and Zimmerman, 8.

10. Linda Main, "Computer Simulation and Library Management," *Journal of Information Science* 13 (1987): 287.

11. Hamon, Weingand, and Zimmerman, 8.

11

Learning to Live in the Twenty-First Century
The Future Starts Now!

The new millennium is knocking at the door. In cartoons, the new year is often depicted as a baby in a diaper, while the old year is drawn as an old man with a long beard, a scythe, and a nearly depleted hourglass. When a *century* ends, that cartoon figure must be old, indeed. In the case of the twentieth century, the magnitude of change has been so significant that the aged man must be nearly bent over with the weight of it!

The new babe, however, whether representative of a year or a century, is bright-eyed and innocent, happy to be here and eager to get on with life. The new century that is almost upon us also carries a positive aura, holding much promise and opportunity—as well as uncertainty and elements of fear. In some ways, the image of the babe could be drawn more accurately as an open doorway through which we must pass in what seems to be a handful of days.

Using another metaphor, in the film *The Wizard of Oz,* Dorothy lived in a black-and-white world until the tornado deposited her in Oz—where the screen bloomed in a riot of color. Carrying that image a bit farther, Dorothy could not enjoy the

160

beauty in which she found herself as she spent all her energies trying to get "home" to that which was known and familiar—even though it was a black-and-white existence. It is a scary proposition to be facing the new and different; what we are used to is so much more comfortable.

Libraries that do not use the opportunities that a changing environment presents face a destiny of declining support. There is a vast difference between the processes of denying, coping, and leading. Libraries that embrace change—and demonstrate leadership to the community through the use of marketing strategies and a future-oriented, proactive focus on the customer—will not only survive into the next century, but thrive!

Building upon a Strong Foundation

Responding to change, however, requires a strong foundation to support the new directions. The California Task Force on the Future of the Library Profession in California, in its report to the California library community, defined three core areas of professional expertise and practice:

> *knowledge of information resources and organization,* including acquisition, storage, and retrieval—the facilitation of access
>
> *understanding of user needs and patterns of information use, and how to match them to information*—professional values such as intellectual freedom are derived from concern for customers and their access to information
>
> *information technology,* the tools with which librarians do their work[1]

This blend of the core areas of information, users, and technology presents a profile of library services as we complete the twentieth century. The Task Force argues that such a congruence distinguishes librarianship from other information providers. Fields such as computer science, communications, and cognitive science address parts of this blend, but only librarianship considers the entire landscape. In fact, it is the wide range of interests possessed by library staff that allows this attention to the broadest interpretation of information work.

The Task Force looks through yet another lens to define the dimensions of practice, dimensions that provide a framework for a more-detailed look at the work that occurs in the information professions. These dimensions include[2]

> *Tool making*   Developing technologies make an increasing variety of tools possible, thereby also altering function: how information is created, distributed, and used. The ability of library staff to establish and maintain a dynamic presence in the public eye in terms of adapting tools to new contexts will determine not only survival but, even more important, centrality.

> *Information management*   The important work of applying tools to the management of information (from acquisition to dissemination) must evolve to a new level. The traditional tools used for information storage, organization, and retrieval must merge with those tools engaged in processes of information access, analysis, and use. The marketing concept of "Place" will simultaneously evolve into one of an "entity" that can be physical, electronic—or other!

> *Service*   Traditional library service has involved the provision of tools to find information and instruction in how to use those tools. However, providing an array of sources does not necessarily include evaluation of those sources in the light of the specific customer need. In the new information universe, users will rely less on the librarian as they turn to machine intermediation; however, there will be more reliance on the librarian for training and as a partner in the information enterprise through analysis, synthesis, and presentation of an information product. In other words, the librarian will serve as an information specialist in partnership with the customer. Such a consulting relationship has been commonly practiced in special libraries, such as those in the legal and medical professions, but less often in other types of libraries. It is important that the service focus

shift from the resource provision model to the consultative model. Increased user training will be an important component of this shift of focus.

Management of information organizations   Issues of management are common to all organizations. Economic constraints that prompt responses of modernization, downsizing, and streamlining are forces that face them as well. Libraries are subject to the same types of pressures, as are their parent organizations. When efficiency, effectiveness, and accountability are mandates for survival and the playing field is complicated by changing conditions, new processes of management and organizational behavior, such as the use of marketing principles and futures methods, need to be explored. It is essential that library managers become knowledgeable about these new processes so that they can help their library organization navigate successfully through the "permanent white water."

If these dimensions of tool making, information management, service, and organizational management are to be both acknowledged and well-handled, library staff need to update their skills continuously, making retooling a top priority. This continuing professional education impetus should be a partnership between library staff as consumers and the multitude of providers, such as graduate library education programs, library and information associations, and private consultants/vendors.

The Forces for Change

Building upon this strong foundation, library staff can move confidently into the new century. But change does not occur in a vacuum. It is usually triggered by one or more destabilizing events that make a new organizational response necessary. In general, these events fall into one or more of the following categories:[3]

> *Shifts in industry structure or product class life cycle*
> Certainly, the information industry is undergoing a major shift in the move from manual to automated systems

and hard copy to electronic form and in the number and variety of "players." The shift is unprecedented in magnitude as it relates to library history and development. Furthermore, it is standard marketing theory that products are "born," develop, peak, decline, and phase out. Throughout this life cycle, changes occur in patterns of demand and users, in needed innovation, and in competition. The library that does not respond to this natural ebb and flow of customer preference, preferring to maintain a traditional profile and operations, will need to be concerned with surviving; thriving is for those libraries that enthusiastically embrace change and customer service.

Technological innovation   The most visible aspect of rapid change today is the rate of technological development. Innovations are occurring daily, and it is a struggle to hang on to the tail of the whirlwind! Technology is forcing change in society, in daily living, in psychological expectations . . . the list goes on and on! Libraries are being transformed by the technologies influencing information storage and retrieval. The key question is whether library staff welcome this transformation in the spirit of a higher level of customer service. Product design needs to be linked with environmental scanning to take advantage of the developments as they occur.

Macroeconomic trends and crises   Such conditions as recession or depression, foreign currencies valuation (affecting the cost of international journals and other publications), and overall economic health of a city/county/state/nation can influence the library's purchase power and level of support. While the library cannot directly influence these megafactors, it is certainly affected by them. Enlightened management uses environmental scanning to develop scenarios depicting a range of possibilities so that plans are in place covering multiple "what if's."

Regulatory and legal changes   Changes in such areas as telecommunications, transportation, and legislation can have immediate effects on the library's delivery of its products and overall funding capacity. Too many library staff members view "politics" in a negative light; they fail to see that it is the process governing the allocation of resources. Every library worker is an ambassador of the library, responsible for educating local, state, and national lawmakers about what the library can provide and what resources are required for doing so. This lobbying effort can influence policymakers so that regulatory and legal decisions are taken based on full knowledge of identified community and library needs. A marketing audit can provide data to support the library's arguments; calculations demonstrating cost-benefit and customer demand are essential.

Market and competitive forces The information industry is expanding, and new competitors are entering the marketplace. This competition may be more aggressive (such as in the case of Internet and cable TV providers) and widespread than has been traditionally encountered by libraries. Marketing-audit data identifying the full range of competitors are critical. Based on this data, decisions should be made regarding the library's appropriate market niche. In addition, if libraries are to become or remain competitive in this volatile market, a commitment to continual improvement of customer service is required.

Growth As organizations become more successful, they may face limitations of size. Community expectations of libraries are now more technologically oriented, and present staff size or expertise may be unable to deal with the growth curve. Furthermore, we must acknowledge that rising circulation does not automatically trigger an increase in staff. Too often, library staff have wonderful and creative plans for meeting more community needs and instituting a higher level of customer service—and bump right into a wall of fiscal resistance from primary funders. Changing intransigent attitudes is difficult but certainly not impossible—particularly if service to these funder/customers is given a high priority. Documentation of the library's response to identified community needs provides a powerful argument. The promotional/commu-

nication message must be one that reports on these identified needs and how the library has responded: The focus
is on benefits.

These forces drive change. Libraries must develop strategies
to cope with the external pressures that are having such profound effect on present and future service—and turn these demands into opportunities!

Dealing with Change

As libraries face the challenges that change presents, a new set
of organizational responses must be developed. Some general
responses that have been suggested in the business literature include the following:[4]

> *Increase quality and customer value.*   Libraries need to
> continually improve the features, performance, reliabil-
> ity, and functionality of the products that they offer to
> their communities. As introduced previously, library
> customers have increasingly more-sophisticated expec-
> tations, and products must be designed that are good
> "matches" with present and anticipated expectations.
> However, employee satisfaction is a strong factor in pro-
> ducing product quality (and, ultimately, customer satis-
> faction) and must be an important consideration when
> designing a process of continuous improvement.
>
> *Decrease the costs of internal coordination.*   This is the
> call for efficiency. To compete successfully, library staff
> need to bring creativity and ingenuity to their analysis of
> internal operations and functions—the internal assess-
> ment portion of the marketing audit—with the intent of
> streamlining processes. However, efficiency must not
> overshadow effectiveness. Product excellence, teamed
> with customer service, is the benchmark against which
> all other efforts must be measured. However, employee
> involvement in developing internal procedures will lead
> to a greater "buy-in" and thereby increase the level of
> employee satisfaction.

Enhance competitive innovation. New initiatives and investments enhance customers' perception of value, particularly when such developments are promoted as addressing identified customer needs. These new products and services can relate to expectations that are either present or latent. If library staff are involved in community groups outside the library, they can more easily monitor customer needs and expectations, resulting in a better competitive position. Using futures methods to explore possibilities can be a real asset to staff planning.

Reduce market-response time. Time is definitely a competitive advantage. It is directly tied to customer convenience factors. If the library can shorten its response time in delivering information to customers, and at a time/location accessible to them, the library's perceived value will be enhanced. When staff and customer convenience factors conflict, it is important to validate the needs of the staff while focusing priorities on external customer concerns. Using marketing and futures principles can aid this effort.

Motivate effective member contributions. The work in libraries is also changing. A key challenge is to empower staff members to contribute in the most productive manner. Both paid and unpaid (volunteer) full-time and part-time staff need to be regarded as full members of the library team. Job descriptions and performance evaluations are essential for all staff. Involving all staff members in marketing/planning and decision making develops a sense of staff ownership in the library's future.

Create scale without mass. A global information society and more competitors within the information industry require a broader scope of staff thinking. Each library is (or should be) its community's window to the world of information. Even when hoped-for resources may not be present and increases in square footage or staff are not realistic, it is important to understand this enlarged scale of thinking and responding to customer inquiries. Staff attitude governs how the library interacts with customers. Staff with futuristic thinking and creativity can more easily connect customers with the information they require.

Manage change at a faster rate.   Paddling a raft through perpetual white water or walking down a street with an earthquake in progress—these metaphors describe today's world of change. Not only is a change environment in libraries real but the periods of disequilibrium seem to come more quickly and last longer. It is becoming important to learn to manage change and to seize the opportunities inherent in every change event. Further, it is important to remember that not only managing the change—but also managing the rate of the change—is instrumental to becoming a proactive organization. Individual staff members will handle the rate of change with different degrees of comfort. In-service training on topics such as stress management, problem solving, and needed technological skills will help staff work effectively in a change environment. Futures strategies—such as Delphi, scenario building, and cross-impact analysis—can help staff gain new insights into change management.

Find true competitive advantage.   Discovering the library's market niche—those products that are better, can be delivered faster, or can be produced more economically than those offered by the competition—is key to a true competitive advantage and success in the marketplace. Today, much is being written in the popular press about how the Internet will make libraries obsolete. This statement ignores the unique and powerful contribution that the library's staff makes in the information transfer process. This human interface between the customer and needed information can, when operating in a proactive and creative environment, offer true value-added service. It could be a very interesting staff development exercise to develop scenarios depicting a world in which the library does—and does not—exist!

Motivating Change

Many people dislike change, and library staff members are no exception to this expression of human nature. However, staff resistance to change can short circuit even the most-progressive management methods. To counter these natural forces that seek to maintain the status quo, strategies for motivating staff must be considered and implemented. The "What's in it for me?" question must be answered with thought and honesty. Similarly, "What's going to happen to me?" is also of deep concern to staff. The resultant anxiety can be extremely disturbing to organizational equilibrium.

Four steps that can be used to motivate employees have been suggested by members of the Delta Consulting Group, a New York-based firm whose practice focuses on the management of strategic organizational change:[5]

> *Identify and surface dissatisfaction with the current state* The known and familiar is always more comfortable and most people are psychologically attached to the current state of affairs. The goal is to jar staff loose from the inertia of the present and to create some willingness to explore the possibilities of change. The greater the uneasiness or discomfort with the present that can be identified, the more interest there will be in investigating change. It can be useful to sketch out the difference between what is and what should be, using data from the marketing audit. Scenario building can also be helpful here:
>
> - a scenario of what would happen if the current state continues unchanged, particularly in light of the current and projected competition
> - scenarios of what the library might be like if various changes were implemented
>
> *Participation in planning and implementing change* Participation increases a sense of ownership. It increases staff excitement, reduces resistance, and motivates employees to make change work. Managers who tend to operate at the more participative end of the authoritarian/participation scale will be more comfortable with this approach than more-traditional managers. Giving up a measure of control can be threatening, but the benefits outweigh the feelings of discomfort. Involving staff

in developing a marketing plan and experimenting with futures methods is important to the library's present and potential effectiveness.

Build in rewards   When desired staff behavior is attained, throughout the process, it is time for both formal and informal rewards that can be liberally dispensed. Such rewards can involve money, promotion, recognition, and status symbols—and should be as closely tied in time to the behavior as possible. Report of staff successes should be part of the library's promotional activities.

Time and opportunity to disengage from the present state   Library staff cannot be expected to embrace change and discard the comfortable state overnight. Feelings of loss, not unlike feelings associated with death and dying, are perfectly normal reactions. Time is needed to mourn the old system. The telling of stories or myths can be a helpful exercise; small group sessions and formal "letting-go" ceremonies are other possibilities. Scenarios can be used to build examples of transitions from current to future states.

These transitions will involve ambiguity, uncertainty, and even fear. Maintaining perspective and giving a full measure of value to what has gone before, stressing the continuity of experience between past and future states, and emphasizing the benefits to be accrued can help maintain a balance and a consistent approach. In addition, if a clear vision is created and clearly understood by all employees, it acts as a lighthouse in the midst of a storm. Attention can be focused on the beam, and the library ship can be accurately steered toward the new shore.

The Need for Vision

The balance of challenges and organizational capacity is best addressed in the context of an overall vision that not only considers today's reality but also dreams of what "might be." When considering the issue of libraries and change, Richard M. Dougherty, professor at the University of Michigan School of Information, proposes that "we librarians are masters at 'talking the talk' of change, but seem to be less skilled at 'walking the walk.'" He strongly argues that library leaders need to "get a grip on change" and "make the change processes work for them, their staffs, and their libraries." Yet, he concludes that most change efforts are incremental and fall "far short of the transformational change most experts feel twenty-first-century organizations must navigate if they are to be successful in the years ahead."[6] Futures methods are not part of the toolbox of most library managers; however, the use of these methods can help them learn to "walk the walk."

Another noted professional, Marilyn Gell Mason, discussed her views of the future of the public library. She made several forecasts in 1985, a number of which have proved to be remarkably accurate. These forecasts included the following:[7]

> *The public library of the future will be judged not by the size of its collections, but by its success in providing information quickly and accurately.* In this changing world, all libraries—not just public libraries—face this challenge. Collection quality and appropriateness have become more important than sheer size. Responding to customer need and convenience with correct information and in a timely way has become a key attribute of accountability and successful performance. Library products must be designed with such goals in mind.

> *Within ten years over half of the service provided to library users will be to individuals who never come into the library.* While technically, we have probably not reached this benchmark as yet, certainly more and more library customers are interacting online with local libraries in terms of searching the catalog, placing holds, and requesting information. Expanding electronic connections and developments are enabling customers to engage library services at a distance. The development of products in an environment of rapid technological change can be aided by the use of environmental scanning and other futures methods.

> *Public libraries will develop an information infrastructure to provide access to a growing and changing flow of information.* The infrastructure of libraries has certainly

changed—and continues to change. A declining number of libraries of all types still operate with manual systems. Electronic resources and linkages are transforming both the look and substance of how libraries operate. Access possibilities are continually expanding, and customer expectations are keeping pace. Marketing principles and futuristic thinking are essential to library effectiveness in developing such an infrastructure.

This infrastructure will include more, smaller library branches.   This forecast is more problematic, as technology has become the overriding impetus for change. However, library substations and kiosks do exist and may well be a trend-to-come as library services evolve. In a sense, each customer's desktop computer could be viewed as a library "branch" as electronic modes of access offer more and more possibilities for gathering information. Focusing on customer service is an important key to success when operating smaller library centers and subcenters.

Levels of service will be developed that will be independent of technology, but will be based instead on staff time required.   Since, in most libraries, staff resources compose 60 to 80 percent of the library's budget, the emphasis on staff time is well placed. In this forecast, technology is regarded as just one of the range of tools available to the librarian in providing service. If the customer is viewed as the core of marketing/planning, these levels can be more effectively developed. The concept of "levels of service" ties neatly to the next forecast, as well.

Fee-based, interactive research services will be developed. When "levels of service" are established, those levels requiring more than a locally identified "basic" level of staff time commitment may be tied to a sliding fee structure. The library defines what "basic" service will be for the community based on information gained in the marketing audit; services beyond this basic level will incur a corresponding charge. While not all libraries have adopted this philosophy, the approach is one that is being increasingly considered by library management.

Futures methods, such as cross-impact analysis and scenario building, can help to clarify the development of these services. Use of the Delphi Method would involve potential customers in the decision making, which is always a desirable activity.

A *new job title of "Information Specialist" will be introduced into the public library.* In the multitude of articles that deal with the image of the librarian, assorted job titles have been suggested over time. Thus far, there has been little evidence that this forecast is becoming mainstream in many libraries. However, in the special library/corporate world, the title has definitely become one that is frequently used. The Delphi Method could bring together the perspectives of librarians and customers in assessing the importance or viability of such a title change.

Book circulation will continue to be an important part of library services. The "death of the book" has also been widely addressed in both popular and library literature. However, there is no indication at this point in history that the book (as traditionally defined) is in immediate danger. Many new technologies continue to be developed and make their contribution to information storage and retrieval. Futures methods can help identify the entrance of technologies into the marketplace and the point at which they can be expected to become mainstream. However, the demise of print culture is not yet occurring. Having said this, the book as a format will "someday" become an artifact joining papyrus rolls and eight-track tapes. But the time is not now.

Public libraries will not only survive, they will flourish. Absolutely! Libraries of all types have the opportunity to thrive and become of increasing importance in the next century. However, an opportunity is not a guarantee, and it is up to library staffs to work toward preferred futures that value customer service. Whatever technologies are or become important to this endeavor must be noted and adopted into library operations.

Dougherty's and Mason's views, together with the additional comments presented, illustrate a core strategy for dealing with a changing environment: Organizations that do survive (and thrive) in the coming decades will be "those that are able to respond quickly and effectively to changing environmental conditions."[8] Attributes that will be needed by these organizations include adaptability, flexibility, risk-taking, and commitment to responsiveness—attributes also important to excellent customer service.

Working toward a Preferred Future

There is one certainty about the future: It will come. It may not be a future that we want, and if we wish to exert any influence on what is to be, working toward a hoped-for future is essential. The flip side of this argument is that equal vigor must be directed against those futures that are not desirable. Without active participation on our part, we cannot criticize the future that emerges because we have done nothing to influence what lies ahead. Figures 11-1 and 11-2 are reproducible worksheets on which to sketch out ideas for the incorporation of marketing and futures strategies in the planning process.

In this book we have considered the elements of marketing and presented each one in tandem with a futures method. This deliberate connection can be useful in linking marketing strategies put in place today with the hoped-for outcomes of tomorrow. Informing the marketing process with futures approaches also helps to define our vision of what the library can be, regardless of the barriers that may need to be scaled. When we plan like the Roman god Janus, looking backward at valuable traditions and forward to challenges and opportunities, we help to establish a seamless transition through turbulent times. The use of marketing as a key managerial process is becoming more widely accepted. Applying the lens of the futurist to this activity can only strengthen the process and enhance the ultimate results.

Figure 11-1   Worksheet: Using Marketing Strategies

Planning Element: *Goal or Objective*	*Marketing Strategy* *That Could Be Helpful*

Figure 11-2   Worksheet: Using Futures Methods

Planning Element: *Goal or Objective*	*Futures Method* *That We Could Use*

THOUGHTS AND MUSINGS

What aspects of a strong foundation can I identify in my library?

What forces of change are presently operating? What forces can I anticipate in the next five years?

How am I dealing with change? What about my library— what change strategies are being tried?

Does my library have a written vision statement? If yes, does it need revising to reflect changing conditions? If no, how can I best help to get such a statement written?

What do I see as the preferred future for my library? Am I actively working toward making it happen?

What are possible futures for my library that would not be advantageous? Am I working to make sure that those future scenarios do not become reality?

Am I thinking like a futurist? Do I consider the potential consequences of my decisions? Do I see the present as one point on a continuum between past and future? How can I become more future-thinking?

Notes

1. "CLA Task Force on the Future of Librarianship" (Sacramento, Calif.: California Library Association, Aug. 1996), 1, 4.
2. "CLA Task Force," 5–7.
3. David A. Nadler and Robert B. Shaw, "Change Leadership: Core Competency for the Twenty-First Century," in David A. Nadler and others, eds., *Discontinuous Change: Leading Organizational Transformation* (San Francisco: Jossey-Bass, 1995), 4–6.

4. Nadler and Shaw, 6–8.

5. David A. Nadler, Robert B. Shaw, A. Elise Walton, and Associates, *Discontinuous Change: Leading Organizational Transformation* (San Francisco: Jossey-Bass, 1995), 51–4.

6. Richard M. Dougherty, "Getting a Grip on Change," *American Libraries* 28, no. 7 (Aug. 1997): 40.

7. Marilyn Gell Mason, "The Future of the Public Library," *Library Journal* 110, no. 14 (1 Sept. 1985): 137–9.

8. Nadler and Shaw, 3.

Further Reading

Adams, Dennis M. *Simulation Games: An Approach to Learning.* Worthington, Ohio: C. A. Jones, 1973.

Albritton, Rosie L., and Thomas W. Shaughnessy. *Developing Leadership Skills: A Source Book for Librarians.* Englewood, Colo.: Libraries Unlimited, 1990.

Ayres, R. *Technological Forecasting and Long Range Planning.* New York: McGraw-Hill, 1969.

Barker, Joel A. *Discovering the Future: The Business of Paradigms.* 2d ed. Burnsville, Minn.: Infinity and Charthouse, 1989. Video.

———. *Paradigm Pioneeers.* Discovering the Future Series. Burnsville, Minn.: Charthouse, 1993. Video.

Barnett, T. "Evaluations of Simulations and Games: A Clarification." *Simulation/Games for Learning* 14, no. 4 (winter 1984): 164–75.

Bennis, Warren, and Michael A. Mische. *The 21st Century Organization: Reinventing through Reengineering.* San Francisco: Jossey-Bass, 1997.

Block, Peter. *The Empowered Manager: Positive Political Skills at Work.* San Francisco: Jossey-Bass, 1989.

Branwyn, Gareth. "Gaming: Simulating Future Realities." *Futurist* 20, no. 1 (Jan.–Feb. 1986): 29–35.

Bright, James R. *Practical Technology Forecasting.* Austin, Tex.: The Industrial Management Center, 1978.

Brodzinski, Frederick R., ed. *Utilizing Futures Research.* San Francisco: Jossey-Bass, 1979.

Bryson, John M. *Strategic Planning for Public and Nonprofit Organizations.* San Francisco: Simon & Schuster, 1995.

"CLA Task Force on the Future of Librarianship." Sacramento: California Library Association, Aug. 1996.

Cornish, Edward. *The Study of the Future.* Washington, D.C.: World Future Society, 1977.

———, ed. *Exploring Your Future: Living, Learning, and Working in the Information Age.* Bethesda, Md.: World Future Society, 1996.

Covey, Stephen R., A. Roger Merrill, and Rebecca R. Merrill. *First Things First.* New York: Simon & Schuster, 1994.

D'Aprix, Roger. *Communicating for Change.* San Francisco: Simon & Schuster, 1996.

Dervin, Brenda. "Useful Theory for Librarianship: Communication, Not Information," *Drexel Library Quarterly* 13, no. 3 (July 1977): 16–32.

Dickson, P. *The Future File: A Guide for People with One Foot in the 21st Century.* New York: Rawson Associates, 1977.

Didsbury, Howard F., Jr. *Student Handbook for the Study of the Future.* Washington, D.C.: 1979.

Dorn, Dean S. "Simulation Games: One More Tool on the Pedagogical Shelf." *Teaching-Sociology* 27, no. 1 (Jan. 1989): 1–18.

Fowles, Jib, ed. *Handbook of Futures Research.* Westport, Conn.: Greenwood, 1978.

Frankl, Viktor E. *Man's Search for Meaning.* New York: Pocket Books, 1959.

Galbraith, Jay R., and Edward E. Lawler III. *Organizing for the Future: The New Logic for Managing Complex Organizations.* San Francisco: Jossey-Bass, 1993.

Giesecke, Joan, ed. *Scenario Planning for Libraries.* Chicago: American Library Assoc., 1998.

Gray, Barbara. *Collaborating: Finding Common Ground for Multiparty Problems.* San Francisco: Jossey-Bass, 1989.

Hamon, Peter, Darlene E. Weingand, and Al Zimmerman. *Budgeting and the Political Process in Libraries: Simulation Games.* Englewood, Colo.: Libraries Unlimited, 1992.

Imparato, Nicholas, and Oren Harari. *Jumping the Curve: Innovation and Strategic Choice in an Age of Transition.* San Francisco: Jossey-Bass, 1996.

Jaffe, Dennis T., Cynthia D. Scott, and Glenn R. Tobe. *Rekindling Commitment: How to Revitalize Yourself, Your Work, and Your Organization.* San Francisco: Jossey-Bass, 1994.

James, Jennifer. *Thinking in the Future Tense.* San Francisco: Simon & Schuster, 1996.

James, Rob, and Jenny Parmenter. "Using Simulation as a Management Training Technique." *Information and Library Manager* 1 (June 1987): 3, 5–7, 9–10.

Kanter, Rosabeth Moss, Barry A. Stein, and Todd D. Jick. *The Challenge of Organizational Change.* San Francisco: Simon & Schuster, 1992.

Kaplan, Robert E. *Beyond Ambition: How Driven Managers Can Lead Better and Live Better.* San Francisco: Jossey-Bass, 1991.

Kotler, Philip. *Marketing for Nonprofit Organizations.* 2d ed. Englewood Cliffs, N.J.: Prentice-Hall, 1982.

Kotler, Philip, and Alan R. Andreasen. *Strategic Marketing for Nonprofit Organizations.* 3d ed. Englewood Cliffs, N.J.: Prentice-Hall, 1987.

Kotter, John P. *A Force for Change: How Leadership Differs from Management.* San Francisco: Simon & Schuster, 1990.

Kouzes, James M., and Barry Z. Posner. *Credibility: How Leaders Gain and Lose It, Why People Demand It.* San Francisco: Simon & Schuster, 1993.

———. *The Leadership Challenge: How to Get Extraordinary Things Done in Organizations.* 2d ed. San Francisco: Simon & Schuster, 1995.

Kubik, George. "Future Views: External Environmental Scanning." *Future Trends* 28, no. 2 (Mar./Apr. 1997): 1.

Linstone, Harold A., and Murray Turoff, eds. *The Delphi Method: Techniques and Applications.* Reading, Mass.: Addison-Wesley, 1975.

Lipman-Blumen, Jean. *The Connective Edge: Leading in an Interdependent World.* San Francisco: Jossey-Bass, 1996.

Main, Linda. "Computer Simulation and Library Management." *Journal of Information Science* 13 (1987): 285–96.

McClure, Charles R., and others. *Planning and Role Setting for Public Libraries: A Manual of Options and Procedures.* Chicago: American Library Assoc., 1987.

Murray, Margo. *Beyond the Myths and Magic of Mentoring.* San Francisco: Jossey-Bass, 1991.

Nadler, David A., and others. *Discontinuous Change: Leading Organizational Transformation.* San Francisco: Jossey-Bass, 1995.

Nadler, Leonard, and Zeace Nadler. *Every Manager's Guide to Human Resource Development.* San Francisco: Jossey-Bass, 1992.

Nanus, Burt. *The Vision Retreat: A Facilitator's Guide.* San Francisco: Jossey-Bass, 1995.

———. *The Vision Retreat: A Participant's Workbook.* San Francisco: Jossey-Bass, 1995.

———. *Visionary Leadership.* San Francisco: Simon & Schuster, 1995.

Noer, David M. *Breaking Free: A Prescription for Personal and Organizational Change.* San Francisco: Simon & Schuster, 1996.

Nonprofit Management and Leadership. Quarterly journal.

O'Toole, James. *Leading Change: Overcoming the Ideology of Comfort and the Tyranny of Custom.* San Francisco: Jossey-Bass, 1995.

Parker, Glenn M. *Team Players and Teamwork.* San Francisco: Simon & Schuster, 1996.

Rosenberg, Philip. *Cost Finding for Public Libraries: A Manager's Handbook.* Chicago: American Library Assoc., 1985.

Schmidt, Warren H., and Jerome P. Finnigan. *The Race without a Finish Line: America's Quest for Total Quality.* San Francisco: Jossey-Bass, 1992.

Tjosvold, Dean. *Teamwork for Customers: Building Organizations That Take Pride in Serving.* San Francisco: Jossey-Bass, 1993.

Toffler, Alvin. *Learning for Tomorrow: The Role of the Future in Education.* New York: Random House, 1974.

Vaill, Peter B. *Learning as a Way of Being: Strategies for Survival in a World of Permanent White Water.* San Francisco: Jossey-Bass, 1996.

Weingand, Darlene E. *Customer Service Excellence: A Concise Guide for Librarians.* Chicago: American Library Assoc., 1997.

———. *Managing Today's Public Library: Blueprint for Change.* (Englewood, Colo.: Libraries Unlimited, 1994.

———. *Marketing/Planning Library and Information Services.* (Littleton, Colo.: Libraries Unlimited, 1987.

———, ed. *Library Trends: Marketing of Library and Information Services* 43, no. 3 (winter 1995).

Zachert, M. J. K. "The Design of Special Library Teaching Tools." *Special Libraries* 64, no. 9 (Sept. 1973): 362.

Zweizig, Douglas, and others. *The Tell It! Manual: The Complete Program for Evaluating Library Performance.* Chicago: American Library Assoc., 1996.

Index

183

Darlene E. Weingand is a professor at the School of Library and Information Studies at the University of Wisconsin–Madison. She is also director of Continuing Education Services.

Weingand has more than eighteen years of experience in training and staff development. She is a certified Myers-Briggs Type Indicator trainer and has taught workshops and seminars both nationally and overseas on marketing, leadership, organizational development, strategic planning, customer services, management, and futures strategies and technologies.

A proponent of continuing education in the library field, she is president of the Continuing Library Education and Exchange Round Table of the American Library Association, a group nationally known for its focus on training and development. She is also active in the International Federation of Library Associations.

Weingand's other ALA books include *Customer Service Excellence: A Concise Guide for Librarians* (1997) and *Administration of the Small Public Library, 3d ed.* (1992). She is the instructor for the 1998 LAMA Institute of the Year on Customer Service Excellence.